Y0-CBC-978

USING TYPE RIGHT

About the Author

For over 35 years Philip Brady has worked with type as a writer, typesetter, editor, and paste-up artist. His career has spanned the printing and newspaper industries and advertising sales and promotion for New England Life, American Optical Company, and Tracerlab. For nine years he taught an annual course for editors of small publications on the basics of type design. Brady uses his experience as a writer (he has written for publications as varied as *The New York Sunday Times* and *Grit*), editor, typesetter, and designer to teach others the fundamentals of using type right.

USING TYPE RIGHT

**121 BASIC
NO-NONSENSE RULES
FOR WORKING
WITH TYPE**

PHILIP BRADY

NTC Business Books

a division of *NTC Publishing Group* • Lincolnwood, Illinois USA

Library of Congress Cataloging-in-Publication Data

Brady, Philip, 1916-
    Using type right/Philip Brady.
        p.   cm.
        Includes index.
    ISBN 0-8442-3375-7
1. Printing, Practical—Layout. 2. Type and type-founding. 3. Graphic arts.
I. Title.
Z246.B73   1988   88-25523
686.2'2—dc19   CIP

First published in hardcover in 1993 by NTC Business Books,
a division of NTC Publishing Group. 4255 West Touhy
Avenue, Lincolnwood (Chicago), Illinois 60646-1975, U.S.A.
© 1988 by Philip Brady. All rights reserved.
First published in softcover by North Light Books,
an imprint of F & W Publications, Inc.
No part of this book may be reproduced, stored in a retrieval
system, or transmitted in any form or by any means.
electronic, mechanical, photocopying, recording or otherwise,
without the prior permission of NTC Publishing Group.
Manufactured in the United States of America.

3 4 5 6 7 8 9 KB 9 8 7 6 5 4 3 2 1

Dedication

Many years of being deeply involved in the hands-on creation, preparation, and production of every variety of graphic material (after graduation from an outstanding school of printing, teaching printing, and ten productive years working at the trade), my career in sales promotion, advertising, and public relations brought me into contact with countless illustrators, graphic designers, printers, engravers, typographers, binders, and paper merchants. From all of them I learned, to them all I owe a deep debt of gratitude. For that reason this book is dedicated to the people of yesterday and today who truly love the printed page, the projected image, the fine art of effective communication in all its graphic forms.

CONTENTS

INTRODUCTION

THIS BOOK WILL HELP you design a magazine, create powerful slides for a sales presentation, produce a sales flip chart, prepare a presentation for the next board of directors meeting, develop a new design for your company stationery, devise or update a company logo, know which way a vertical book page should face, and understand why two hyphens do not an em dash make.

It will teach you enough about the basics of typographic design (and production) so you'll be able to spot both the unwise and the unworkable. It will enable you to reject the "everyone on Madison Avenue is now using Optima so we should, too" way of thinking.

Regardless of the typesetting method you use, regardless of whether you plan to print by offset, gravure, silk screen, letterpress, or laser, the information in this book will be valid. The principles and practices discussed here apply to the "up front" procedures used to prepare graphic materials, so they'll hold true no matter what technology you use. They will never grow old, for they are basics, time-proven and universal in application.

A knowledge of basic design is always helpful because once you know the fundamentals, you'll know when rules may be broken without doing harm to the final design.

You should remember that rules *can* be broken or dodged. What makes any design right or wrong for you, your company, or your client is its impact on the recipient. The only real rule is that the unspoken message conveyed through all the project's design elements must be the correct one. So learn the basic rules laid out in this book, then use them to develop your own sense of design.

I'd like you to recommend this book to your friends. That's important, for among us we can promote the correct, the good, as opposed to the mediocre—which is always available in abundance. By learning the basics, studying good typography, and sharing what we learn with one another, we can help maintain high standards for using type.

Here's a hint for using this book: Keep a type specimen book handy as you read. If you're not familiar with a typeface that's mentioned, look at the sample in the specimen book, then compare it to other typefaces mentioned and to illustrations within this book. That way you'll begin to learn the specific attributes and characteristics of many useful, well-designed typefaces and can put them to work for you.

PART ONE

DESIGNING WITH TYPE

A NEWSPAPER headline set all caps, in 120-point bold type, and splashed across the top of page one, simply shrieks at you. You can't help but read it. That's because it makes good use of *visual signals.* Its size, boldness, capital letters, and position on the page are all signals that make you take notice.

Visual signals is my term for the hundreds of design and type elements that determine how well the message—the thoughts in the head of the writer—is transferred into the head of the reader. Good, clear signals help the reader grasp the message quickly. Improper, fuzzy signals hinder the reader, regardless of the medium used to present the message.

Designing with type means controlling all the visual signals so *how* a typeset piece *looks* reinforces what it *says.* Whether you're designing the piece yourself or overseeing the work of a designer, once you begin to think seriously about the many things you can do to prepare an advertisement, a page of type, a 35mm slide, a company logotype, or the cover of a brochure so that all the elements increase readership and comprehension, you'll be well on the way to mastering the most important concept of designing with type.

WHAT IS A SIGNAL?

An elementary example of a signal is the indentation at the beginning of a paragraph. It says to the reader, "This is a new paragraph." That small space is a signal we all recognize and respond to swiftly, without conscious thought.

Punctuation is also a signal. A period signals the end of a sentence. An exclamation mark also ends a sentence, but sends a far different message.

White space can also be used as a signal. The size of the type selected for headlines, the spacing—and placing—of elements on a page, the number of lines in a heading, whether the heads are one, two, or more columns wide—all are signals.

The choice of paper, ink and paper colors, layout style, illustration technique, typefaces—all are important signals.

Did you raise your eyebrows at some of the items mentioned? Literally no element that goes into creating a visual message—whether it's a book, brochure, broadside ad, or color slide—is neutral. Each element is a signal acting as either a friend or a foe to getting the message across.

THE SUBTLETY OF SIGNALS

You've probably noticed you tune out messages you wish to ignore in printed material—often much of the advertising. In the same way you unconsciously tune out some signals, you absorb others without realizing it, responding to them as you should, and integrating them into your understanding of the message being presented.

If a news story on the front page of your daily newspaper is below the fold (that is, on the bottom half of the page), you understand—even if you've never been told—it is less important than those stories appearing above the fold.

At the same time, you realize that since it appears on page one, it's more important than the stories inside.

So while signals can be very subtle, their impact on the message can be critical. The more good, clear signals, the smoother the transfer of the message from paper or film to the reader's brain. The more murky or misleading the signals, the greater the handicap imposed.

MISLEADING AND UNNEEDED SIGNALS

Despite their importance, signals are often used badly. Some glaring examples of bad signals you may have seen before are: credits and captions printed over a background photo of foaming surf, black letters superimposed on a dark background, white letters against a pale sky.

Improper typeface selection, or at least uninformed type selection, can result in more of these "minus" signals. It's not uncommon to see fine designs that suffer from the use of ho-hum text or display faces. Such designs, many times, could have been knockouts if a text face with character had been used to increase overall design impact. An example? Times Roman is a fine, legible face but it has no special character. When replaced by Trump, Palatino, Garamond, or Goudy, to name only a few fine choices, the character enhancement can be tremendous.

A study of almost any magazine you pick up will reveal literally hundreds of signals that interfere with the message. And they appear in headlines, text, and advertising alike. Too harsh an indictment? Once you become aware of signals, and their importance, make the test for yourself. You can't fail to note so many graphic illiteracies you'll be totally convinced.

Unnecessary signals can slow readership as much as incorrect signals do. One such signal, in use for far too long, is now being eliminated. I'm referring to the indentation at the beginning of a paragraph following a head or subhead. The reader, having no other place to start reading, has no need for a signal saying, "Here's the beginning of the next paragraph."

When multiplied, unneeded signals slow down the reader by requiring him or her to process additional information. In this case, the space also creates a ragged left-hand line, where a smooth alignment of headlines and text would add to the beauty of the page. And the paragraph space costs money, since it requires one extra keystroke, multiplied by every head and subhead in your publication.

JOB TIPS

Here are a few tips to help you succeed in your career. For more information on getting ahead, review the material in Chapter 2, pages 86 - 109.

Starting a New Job

- Don't criticize or make suggestions until you know the company dynamics (3-6 months).
- Don't underestimate the power of lower-level staff members. Secretaries and assistants can be valuable.
- Study interactions. While several people may have the same rank, often one emerges as the leader. You can learn who that person is only by paying attention.

Staying Put

- Choose an image and project it in everything you do—through the logo you use on stationery to the color of your clothes.
- Don't get too close to your coworkers. When you're promoted, such friendships can make management difficult.
- Make sure your posture, movements and gestures convey assurance. If you have nervous hands, put them in your pockets. Walk confidently, speak slowly.

Several misleading or unneeded signals hinder the message here. The extra space beneath the headings separates the subheads from their text, the oversized bullets draw too much attention to themselves, and there's no need for the indent after the major head. Subtle mistakes such as these can hinder communication.

FOUR MAJOR SIGNALS

While every element in a printed brochure, slide presentation, or flip chart either enhances or lessens the impact you are striving to create, four key elements are so important that missing on any one will doom a project—even if the other three are right.

These four signals are typeface, layout, paper selection, and use of color.

All four are critical. A typeface that's hard to read, a poor design, the wrong paper, an ill-chosen ink color . . . all are equally damaging. None of these elements can be ignored or misused.

Typeface: When choosing a typeface, you must consider both *character* and *legibility*. Frederic W. Goudy, one of America's greatest and most prolific type designers, described character this way: "Character in types has to do with the impression made by the individual forms, their proportions, and the intangible something in them that makes the letters of each word hang together to form an agreeable whole; each letter with a quality of completeness, and not made up of bits taken here and there; each a shape with an air of its own, *with graces not too obvious*, and with no affectation of antiquity." (Italics are mine.)

In this book, I'll use *character* to refer to the personality or mood that a particular typeface projects, whether it is modern or old-fashioned, bold or subtle, plain-spoken or elaborate.

Legibility is related to the speed with which each letter or letter combination—that is, each word—can be recognized. Don't confuse this with *readability*. Readability is the relative ease with which you can read a printed page due to type arrangement, page design, spacing between elements— in other words, the overall appearance of the entire piece.

To appreciate legibility more, take a sheet of paper and cover the bottom half of the letters in several words. What can you read? Try this experiment with a line of upper- and lowercase letters and with one having only caps.

Repeat the action, but this time allow only the base of the letters to show. Again, can you read the words? How readily? All the parts of a letter, including the serifs, are important to legibility, but the tops seem relatively more important.

Most of us learned to read using textbooks printed with a roman typeface, often Century Schoolbook (which although very legible is hardly beautiful—a real plain Jane). So we're conditioned to read most easily lowercase letterforms with moderately thick and thin elements, and serifs. Keep this in mind when choosing a typeface. All-cap lines, Gothic faces, sans serif types, and italic text tend to be less legible.

Typography
Avant Garde Book

Modern, stylish, high-tech.

Typography
Helvetica

Same as above.

Typography
Century Schoolbook

Plain, legible, sensible.

Typography
Bodoni Book

Modern, crisp, sharp.

Typography
Cheltenham Old Style

Rugged, strong.

Typography
Garamond

Classic, legible, dainty, dignified.

Typography
Goudy Old Style

Dignified, classic.

Typography
Weiss

Modern, classic.

Typography
Palatino

Same as Weiss.

Typography
Souvenir Light

Modern, light-hearted,
a bit rugged.

Typography
Times Roman

News, legible, plain. (Large x-
height.)

Typography
Trump

Modern, classic, graceful.

Each typeface has its own personality, and it's important that you
choose one that's appropriate for
your message.

Process lettering from Typographic House Inc., Boston.

Layout: You must have absolutely the right layout in terms of the image your company or organization wants to project, the product or service being sold, the audience being romanced. A simple, clean, well-structured layout will lead the reader into and through the piece.

The simple and clean will win out every time over a complex, cluttered presentation.

There are two primary ways that layout gives the reader signals that either help or hinder. The first is positioning.

Look at the morning newspaper again. The fact that a story is on page one says it's important. That's positioning. The fact that it's at the top of the page says it's the most important story that day. That's also positioning. Positioning is a strong visual signal, one we grasp and understand from long conditioning, without conscious thought.

The second way layout gives the reader signals is through the use of white space. Unfortunately, this is one signal that is often not used well. Why? Simply because the designer or paste-up artist (the person who assembles the elements on the page) doesn't always understand the function of white space and the important signals it can send to the reader.

One key to using white space effectively is to understand that the reader's eye is intuitively attracted to white, so elements with a lot of space around them get more attention. The reader perceives elements spaced closely together as being connected and those spaced apart as separate. Thus, the correct use of white space is vital to any printed piece.

Paper and use of color: The paper stock must be right—not neutral, but positive, adding as much as possible to your message. This means you must use a paper of the right color and weight, compatible with the ink, reinforcing your basic message. You must also select the proper ink colors, the amount of color used, the items to be in color.

Not only must the paper color be right, but you must never overlook how texture, surface appearance, and feel of the printed sheet can reinforce your message. A booklet printed on white mimeo paper, for example, can never equal the character message imparted by the use of a fine, 70-pound, white laid sheet. The tactile feel alone is worth its extra cost.

Another example of poor paper selection? A sheet of inexpensive white stock used for a letterhead, versus the positive impact of the same letterhead on 100 percent rag stock.

KEEP IT CONSISTENT

The final consideration when designing a typeset piece is consistency. As you make and carry out all the decisions we just discussed, aim for consistency in spacing, head treatment, type selection, layout. Every style element should be faithfully correct from page one to the end of the project.

By establishing the proper signals on page one and then maintaining them, you'll ensure that readers quickly learn the signals and automatically react to them throughout the balance of your publication.

Consistency also includes the projection of a consistent image of the company or product through every graphic element reaching the public. Every design must be guided by the same philosophy, so each new item reinforces the previous messages, one building on the other.

MANY TRIFLES MAKE PERFECTION

This might be a good place to introduce one of my favorite quotations. It was coined by the Shakers, I believe. If you know and appreciate the clean, lean lines of their furniture, you'll be delighted with the quote's aptness. Think about:

> "Many trifles make perfection,
> but perfection is no trifle."

CHAPTER 1

The Creative Aspects of Design

DESIGNING WITH TYPE means, literally, using typography to transfer a message from one person to another. As we've just seen, this involves hundreds of subtle signals, from the difference between a period and an exclamation point to indicate the end of a sentence, to the feel and weight of the paper stock.

In this chapter, I'll focus on the creative considerations of design, ranging from how to choose typefaces for display and text type to how to decide what size type to use.

1. Determine the character you want to project

Your firm or organization, like every other, has (or should have) a character it wishes to project, and *all* your graphic materials should project that character. So you must determine exactly what that character is before you can create or buy graphic designs that deliver the right message.

Determining your organization's character is the most critical step you'll take when starting to design a printed piece. Sit down and make a list of the attributes your firm has or should project. Get those who'll approve the final piece to agree on these attributes, then keep them in mind as you choose a typeface, paper, and ink, and lay out the piece.

THE KENDALL WHALING MUSEUM
27 Everett Street ✆ P.O. Box 297
Sharon, Massachusetts 02067

Stuart M. Frank, Director   Telephone: (617) 784-5642

©1984 by Kendall Whaling Museum, Sharon, MA 02067 USA. Designed by Stuart M. Frank; produced and printed by CopyTech, Stoughton, MA. Used by permission.

These designs project dramatically different characters. The Kendall Whaling Museum stationery—with dark gray ink, linen-finish stock, period illustration, classic roman typeface, and traditional design—gives a sense of history. The Sedia ad, on the other hand, uses clean, sleek type and artwork to evoke a much more modern look.

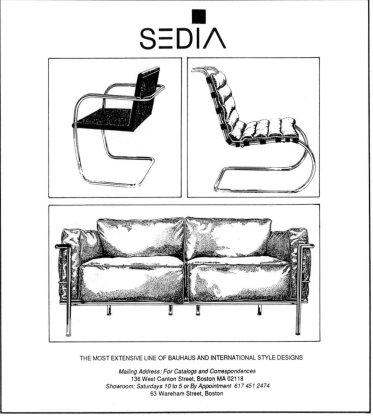

THE MOST EXTENSIVE LINE OF BAUHAUS AND INTERNATIONAL STYLE DESIGNS

Mailing Address: For Catalogs and Correspondences
136 West Canton Street, Boston MA 02118
Showroom: Saturdays 10 to 5 or By Appointment 617 451 2474
63 Wareham Street, Boston

©1987 by Sedia, Inc. International Style Furniture advertisement courtesy of Sedia, Inc.

2. Know your audience

No printed item can be designed, no typeface selected, unless you know the audience you will be addressing. For example, Trafton Script, a dainty face, will not impress foundry owners; Stymie Bold will not sweep owners of gift shops off their feet. If your audience will be either very young or very old, use a larger text type so it can be read more easily. If you're appealing to busy executives, you should give important elements enough emphasis to be seen even by someone quickly scanning the page.

The type choices in these two pieces show they are directed at two very different audiences. The Pressto logo, with its clean, sharp typeface and fanfold illustration, is designed to appeal to people who use computer forms. It communicates speed and efficiency. The Hotel Meridien ad, aimed at an up-scale audience, is sophisticated and classy.

MEET with SUCCESS.

When you plan your meeting at the Hotel Meridien, no detail that will make it a complete success is overlooked.

There are several size rooms. All impeccably appointed. With everything you require, right down to the pads and pencils.

Trust our chefs to strike the perfect culinary note. And each staff member to be assiduously yet unobtrusively attentive.

There is perhaps no finer setting in which to meet with success.

Right here in the heart of Boston. The Hotel Meridien.

Reservations and Information:
617-451-1900

HOTEL
MERIDIEN
Travel companion of Air France.

Private valet parking. 250 Franklin St., Boston

Used by permission of Ken Maryanski, Le Meridien Hotel Boston. Art Illustration: Ken Maryanski.

Courtesy of Data Forms Co. Inc.

3. Match the typeface to the message

Every typeface has a character that either helps to deliver your message, harms the delivery, or is neutral. Once you've determined the kind of character your printed message must possess to be most effective, select a typeface to match.

You can recognize character easily in some faces; it's very subtle in others. There are masculine, feminine, delicate, rugged, Victorian, Colonial (and many other period faces), avant-garde, formal, informal, high-tech, Oriental faces. The variety of characters is almost as endless as the faces available.

For example, Eve, with its special caps and ascenders, is the epitome of a feminine typeface; Caslon Antique's Colonial look conveys a sense of the historic; the elaborate Cloister Black is perfect for the ecclesiastical look; and Japanette gives a feeling of the Orient.

Each of these typefaces reinforces the written message. Americana has a "Fourth of July" kind of feeling; Shelley Andante is calligraphic; Serif Gothic Light adds to the airy quality; Futura Extra Bold Condensed has a heavy solidity.

Enjoy America's Early Heritage

A Pen for People Who Love to Write

Dine in our light, airy sunroom

Our advice is rock solid

4. Decide how many typefaces to use

Some typography experts say that no piece should use more than two type-faces or families, but you shouldn't feel confined by such an arbitrary rule. There are times when one type family is sufficient and times when more than two typefaces can be useful. An example of the latter: a department store catalog, where one page offers Christmas items such as creches. It certainly would be appropriate to use a type such as Wedding Text or Old English for heads on this page, even though your basic head style throughout the catalog was entirely different.

When deciding how many faces to use, remember that the point of using different faces is to achieve some differentiation between, for example, text and heads. Different faces can also add some variety to your project, make it look more interesting. If a piece has very little text, you may not need the variety of more than one type, and you may choose to keep it all in one family. If the project has a lot of text or needs to project more than one character, as in the catalog mentioned above, you may need more than the usual two faces.

Be careful, though. The use of a mixture of faces in one project is tricky and should be left to seasoned professionals who know how and when to mix faces. Each typeface sends a different message, and you don't want to confuse the reader by sending too many messages—some of which may well be conflicting.

The Kohler Co., successfully, uses only the popular Futura family to provide a clean, modern look. The combination of just two faces, a sans serif face for heads and a serif for text, works well for *Publishers Weekly*.

THE BOLD LOOK
OF **KOHLER**

The Thunder™ Grey of a rainstorm. The Tender™ Grey of dawn. Two beautiful new greys from Kohler. Let them bring strength or delicacy to your bath or powder room. To find out where and how, see the Yellow Pages for the local Kohler Showroom in your area, or send $2 to Kohler Co., Dept. AH0, Kohler, Wisconsin 53044.

C5049 Copyright 1985 Kohler Co.

Courtesy of Kohler Co.

Bantam Keeping *Sinatra* Pub Date Under Wraps

Though Bantam Books announced an "on sale" date of July 23 for Kitty Kelley's unauthorized biography of singer Frank Sinatra in its spring 1986 catalogue, the company now says that "we

Charles R. Longsworth
President

You Are Cordially Invited
To Participate In The
Restoration Of
Colonial Williamsburg

Dear Friend,

Imagine, if you will, these scenes from America's past:

- Thomas Jefferson, as a young student,
  poring over law books in the company
  of his friend and mentor, George Wythe;

- Patrick Henry thundering his defiance
  of King George III;

- George Washington, a member of Virginia's
  House of Burgesses, dining with friends
  at the Raleigh Tavern and discussing plans
  that would eventually lead to the birth of
  a new republic.

You can use just one type family
or you can mix families, if you do
so carefully. The Colonial Williamsburg Foundation successfully uses
a mixture of typefaces.

Reprinted by permission of The Colonial Williamsburg Foundation.

5. When using two families, don't team similar faces

When you set headlines and text in two different faces, make sure they *really* are different. Don't ever use two faces that look very much alike. If the two faces are so similar that the reader can't tell them apart, why bother using two faces? Since the point of using two different faces is to draw some distinction between different type elements, using look-alike faces defeats the purpose.

Instead, try mixing a serif text face and a sans serif head, or vice versa. For example, Helvetica headlines and Palatino text . . . fine. The combination won't confuse the reader and may well add visual liveliness to the printed piece. Palatino headlines and Helvetica text . . . also fine, although we do not read sans serif text as easily as we do a serif face.

Quick type tip: How do you pick the right combination? Here's a quick way to tell how two faces will work together. Make photostats of a patch of the display type you wish to try and a few lines of the desired text, using a type manual. Cut and paste the two patches together to simulate a head over text. You can't read the copy, of course, but you can very easily "see" the color, size, and type relationships.

These two faces are so much alike that there's little distinction between heads and text. Instead of teaming two similar faces (like the Helvetica and Universal used here), try mixing a sans serif face with a serif.

Promotions
Alice Henderson, who has been assistant bookkeeper since 1982, has been promoted to assistant director of the accounting department. Alice has been with the company since 1979.

Did you know?
One of our own has been named chairman of the local United Way campaign for this year. James Neilsen of the finance department will head up the drive. See next month's *In House* for a full article on this fine program and its goals.

Hot off the press
A new book about where to go and what to do when visiting Los Angeles has just hit the newsstands, and it was written by none other than

6. When using one family, choose a flexible one

Mixing typefaces must be done with informed discretion to avoid pairing non-compatible faces. An inexperienced designer may choose two typefaces that convey conflicting messages, such as pairing a sleek, modern face with one of the black-letter faces based on ancient handwriting. This will confuse the character message you are trying to send to the reader.

To avoid such problems, you may choose to stick to one type family for both display and text.

If you do, make sure you select a family with a lot of flexibility. That way you can achieve every bit of the variety required for your particular project without having to worry about whether the types go well together.

One good example of a type family with flexibility is Helvetica, which includes such variations as Helvetica **Bold**, Light, *Light Italic*, Regular, Regular Condensed, Expanded, and Outline. With so many choices, Helvetica easily can be used to advantage for both text and display.

Some typefaces offer additional flexibility through features such as small capitals and swash letters, as in Caslon Old Style.

The type family you choose must be flexible if you're going to rely on it for an entire design. This sales brochure beautifully demonstrates how a lot of variety can be achieved with just one family—Goudy.

On this tour, we should see some 200 species of birds, including Yellow-bellied Flycatcher, Black-backed and Three-toed Woodpeckers, Arctic Tern, all three jaegers, Sabine's and Little Gulls, both redpolls, Harris' Sparrow, Common Eider, Bohemian Waxwing, Northern Shrike, Red-necked Grebe, Baird's, LeConte's and Sharp-tailed Sparrows, Sprague's Pipit, Chestnut-collared Longspur, Connecticut Warbler, Boreal Chickadee and Gray Jay. Previous tours have watched active nests of Horned Grebe, Willow Ptarmigan, Red-necked Phalarope, Stilt Sandpiper, Red Crossbill, Three-toed Woodpecker, Mew Gull, Northern Shrike, and the beautiful rosy-breasted Ross' Gull.

LEADERS
I: Kim Eckert and Dale Delaney
II: Victor Emanuel and Greg Lasley
LIMIT: 16
FEE: $1675. from Winnipeg

Detailed itineraries available upon request

NORTHEASTERN MINNESOTA/ NORTH DAKOTA
June 18–27, 1988

A summer tour in northeastern Minnesota promises a wealth of activity for birders. The boreal forests and bogs of this area are home to many highly sought after birds, as well as a multitude of more familiar species in full song, full breeding plumage and in characteristic nesting habitat. Black-backed Woodpecker, Boreal Chickadee and Ruffed Grouse are widespread residents of this beautiful countryside; Least, Alder and Yellow-bellied Flycatchers, and more than 20 species of warblers, including Connecticut, Cape May and Mourning, will be at their vocal best; Yellow Rails, Sharp-tailed and Le Conte's Sparrows abound in a favored sedge marsh; and, Sharp-tailed Grouse are found in a nearby field. With luck, we might even see nesting Spruce Grouse, Boreal, Great Gray or Northern Saw-whet Owls.

Native prairie is one of the most threatened habitats in North America, but in North Dakota near Jamestown one can still find magnificent grassland and undisturbed pothole lakes. Here we will seek the rare Baird's Sparrow, marvel at the flight song of the Sprague's Pipit, and observe Greater Prairie-Chicken, Gray Partridge, Ferruginous Hawk, Chestnut-collared Longspur and other interesting prairie breeders. The sweeping grasslands of the northern Great Plains offer expansive vistas and a rewarding end to our birding expedition.

LEADER: Kim Eckert. A second leader will be added as tour size warrants.
LIMIT: 16
FEE: $995. from Duluth

Detailed itineraries available upon request

POINT PELEE AND THE KIRTLAND'S WARBLER
May 7–16, 1988

Predictable, yet puzzling and mysterious, the spectacle of avian migration is among the most fascinating in nature. Each spring and fall, we witness the passage of tens of thousands of birds—the distances they travel are often vast, the path beset with the hardships of an unyielding environment.

Point Pelee has long been famous as one of the most remarkable migration concentration points in North America. Extending some nine miles into the western end of Lake Erie, the Point represents a funnel of land which birds follow on their way south in the fall, and the first available land to be reached on their spring flight north. The great variety of habitats in the relatively small Point Pelee area further increases the species diversity and actual numbers of birds using the Point as a stopover.

Mid-May is the most exciting time of year to be at Point Pelee. If weather conditions are good, the concentration of grounded migrants will provide some of the most thrilling birding in North America. The woods north of the tip can be teeming with hundreds of warblers, vireos, orioles,

Kirtland's Warbler
Dendroica kirtlandii

tanagers, flycatchers, grosbeaks, buntings, thrushes, and others on their way north with the spring. Species which perform diurnal migrations—herons, hawks, some shorebirds, gulls, terns, and swallows—move north over the tip all day. The fervor of the season is high as these birds near their summer destinations, and the morning chorus at Point Pelee is among North America's finest.

Following our stay at Point Pelee, we will travel to the jack-pine forests of north-central Michigan in search of the endangered Kirtland's Warbler on its breeding grounds.

LEADER: Steve Hilty & Kim Eckert
LIMIT: 16
FEE: $1095. from Detroit

Detailed itineraries available upon request

Courtesy of Victor Emanuel Nature Tours; Paul Donahue, artist, and Roberta Hill, brochure designer.

7. Trust typefaces that are tried and true

Some typefaces are so versatile that they can be used time after time for a variety of applications. If you're familiar with these faces and know how to manipulate them for a range of effects, you can handle almost any type problem. A few of the reliables are Goudy, Bodoni, and Garamond, among older faces, and Trump, Melior, and Palatino for newer designs.

Come on down to Jack Daniel's someday and watch us make our smooth-sippin' whiskey.

AGING A BATCH of Jack Daniel's calls for years of time and no small amount of footwork.

There are thousands of charred oak barrels in a ten-story warehouse. Full up, each barrel is too heavy to lift. So to get the whiskey properly maturing, our barrelmen need to kick them into place. If you ever tried to boot a 400 pound barrel, you'd know what these gentlemen are up against. But after a sip of properly aged Jack Daniel's, you'll be glad they're so fancy with their feet.

SMOOTH SIPPIN'
TENNESSEE WHISKEY

Tennessee Whiskey•80-90 Proof•Distilled and Bottled by Jack Daniel Distillery
Lem Motlow, Proprietor, Route 1, Lynchburg (Pop. 361), Tennessee 37352

Permission granted by Jack Daniel Distillery.

Frederic Goudy's classically beautiful Italian Old Style provides the desired character for this Jack Daniel's ad. If you stick with proven typefaces like this, you can't go wrong.

8. Use display type to convey character

If both the display type (type that's bigger or bolder than the basic text type) and the text face have strong characters, the two can conflict with each other. To prevent this, your text face can be neutral and the desired character imparted by headlines and other display type.

Using display type to convey character may work better than using a very distinctive text type for two reasons: First, since the display type is larger, the reader gets a sense of the character immediately. Second, some of the more distinctive typefaces used to establish a personality may be difficult to read when used as text.

Boston's First International Nightclub
The Fashion. The Touch. The Sensation.
Sheer Beauty in any Language From a Sensuous Whisper
To an Explosion of Color and Sound.
Open at 8:00 PM Thursday, Friday, Saturday
Ron Della Chiesa, host
Reservations, call 236-8788 or 236-1100
at the Back Bay Hilton
40 Dalton Street, Boston
Valet garage parking available

Used by permission of Back Bay Hilton, 40 Dalton Street, Boston, MA 02115.

Notice how these two ads use display type to set the mood. The ad for Le Papillon uses a hand-lettered heading that captures the international flavor, and an "old but new" character comes through very well in the Barn Masters, Inc. ad. The body type in each ad is much less elaborate than the display type.

We restore Post and Beam

John Libby builds and restores post and beam barns and period structures maintaining authentic detailing and original integrity. Consulting, inspections, and detailed reports are part of our service.

BARN Masters Inc.
Quality Homes and Post and Beam Structures
Consultation and Reports
Upper Pleasant Street, Freeport, Maine 04032
207/865-4169

Barns by JOhN Libby est. 1971

Used by permission of Barn Masters, Inc. All rights reserved.

19

9. Avoid fancy faces

While you want type that is distinctive, don't choose a typeface that's too elaborate. Fancy typefaces can be very hard to read. In some, a heading of one or two words might work, but more can be a disaster. Such faces usually can't be set in all caps. As shown here, *Bonanza* is barely legible and *Congratulations* doesn't work at all.

The words *Bonanza,* set in Crayonette, and *Congratulations,* set in Murray Hill Bold show why you should be careful with fancy faces.

BONANZA

CONGRATULATIONS

10. Watch out for "unruly" characters

The key to a well-designed typeface lies in the "fit" of the characters, each one with all others. Good design also appears in the harmony with which letterforms work together, each supporting the others without calling undue attention to itself. Any typeface with "busy" characters should be used with caution. These busy letters sometimes can impede legibility and annoy readers, and today's reader has neither time nor tolerance for visual annoyance.

Goudy said it this way: "When a type design is good it is not because each individual letter of the alphabet is perfect in form, but because there is a feeling of harmony and unbroken rhythm that runs through the whole design, each letter kin to every other and to all."

Because fit and harmony are so important, Goudy learned to cut the punches and dies needed to cast his types, all to insure maximum fit and to retain his design subtleties. A fine example is his Goudy Handtooled series.

On the other hand, note the lowercase *h, d, g,* and *s* in Chesterfield and their impact. Faces such as this can be used wisely for character in short headings, but shouldn't be used extensively.

Busy characters such as the *g, h, s, y,* and *d* in this typeface produce visual distraction. One or two such letters in a short heading may add spice, but in text they would be murder.

"The high dedication to 'systems' idols"

11. Some faces can't be set in all caps

A prime example of a typeface that can't be set all caps is a face almost always referred to as Old English, whether the designation is correct or not. Here's a sample recently clipped from a newspaper advertisement. Doesn't work, does it? The word *Easter* is set in Old English. The adjoining horrible example is set in Typo Script and spells *gardens*. Would you be able to identify the last character as a cap *S* if you saw it standing alone?

Many typefaces, such as black-letter and script faces, shouldn't be set in caps, but often are. Here are two examples from newspaper advertisements. Don't work, do they?

12. Don't set large blocks of text in italic or bold

Try not to set a great deal of text in upper and lowercase italic, particularly if you're using small sizes or a face with fine elements, such as Caslon. Such text can be weak and hard to read. Roman text is almost always a better bet. If you need italic text, select a sturdy italic such as Trump.

Also, the letters in italic all-cap lines tend to fit badly (unless they are very carefully spaced, visually, by an expert) and thus are more difficult to read.

Large blocks of text in boldface also should be avoided, since they're usually too heavy, too black, and not friendly.

Large blocks of italic type like this one tend to be weak and not as legible as roman. In most cases, use roman for text and save italic or bold for emphasis.

> *The new equipment will allow us to provide speedier service for our 6,000 mail-order customers, as well as help us track inventory and improve processing of buyer orders. It will arrive in three months and be up and running by the end of the year.*
>
> *Known as the ST-1543, the system has more than three times the capacity of our current equipment and provides many more functions. Among the new features are:*

13. Look at a bold typeface carefully before using it

When you examine the bold or ultra-bold varieties of a particular face, you will often find that some or all of the grace and beauty of the roman has been lost. What you gain in boldness may not be worth the loss in character. So consider other means to give emphasis, such as using a larger size or color.

If you *must* use a bold typeface for a particular design, choose one that retains the beauty of its companion roman.

Condensed or expanded versions of a particular typeface also can lose much of the basic family character. Unless you *must* squeeze or expand type to fill a specified measure, consider carefully before using such versions.

14. Be weight conscious

Weight, or *color*, refers to the visual impact of a body of type, say a book page. Set in one typeface, a page might appear black, in another, gray. For example, even a few lines of Caslon Old Style and Bookman are adequate to reveal their weight difference.

Weight is important to the message you're trying to convey. A booklet on children's clothing set in a relatively heavy face, such as Bookman, may well be too dark, too funereal for the topic discussed. Set in Garamond or Trump, it could be light and pleasant, wholly inviting to the reader.

With many text faces, weight or color is easy to predict. To help you, the better specimen books include blocks of type of the most popular text faces. However, unless you know your typefaces very well, you might be unpleasantly surprised if you don't carefully check the weight of a face before choosing it for an important project. When weight is critical, set and compare several test pages.

Another way to control or vary weight is to use tracking. With tracking, you create text with different colors by using different degrees of spacing between characters. The more letterspacing, the lighter the color.

The top sample is set in 10-point Caslon #37, the bottom in 10-point Bookman. You can see that even though the leading is equal, the Bookman has a darker color.

HE took his ship away. The affair was not discussed at home, though each of us gave it some private despondency. We followed him silently, apprehensively, through the reports in the *Shipping Gazette*. He made point after point safely — St. Vincent, Gibraltar, Suez, Aden — after him we went across to Colombo, Singapore, and at length we learned that he was safe at Batavia. He had got

He took his ship away. The affair was not discussed at home, though each of us gave it some private despondency. We followed him silently, apprehensively, through the reports in the Shipping Gazette. He made point after point safely — St. Vincent, Gibraltar, Suez, Aden — after him we went across to Colombo, Singapore, and at length we learned that he was safe

Courtesy of Composing Room of New England.

15. Carefully consider character count

If you are selecting a text face for a printed piece with lots of copy, the number of characters per line may be critical. The more characters per line, the fewer the pages to print and handle, and the lower the costs.

Type specimen books often provide the character count per pica of all text faces. Or you can measure a lowercase alphabet in the size you plan to use.

The differences between character counts of typefaces of the same point size can be significant. In one specimen book, 10-point Garamond Book gets 2.68 characters per pica; Kennerly, 2.76 characters per pica; and Modern, 2.29. Sure, it seems like a small difference, but think in terms of a 5½" × 8" book of 100,000 words. It could be as much as 55 pages longer set in Modern than in Kennerly!

Different typefaces take up different amounts of space, which can be important if you're setting large amounts of text. The difference in character count between 12-point Cloister, Goudy, and Garamond is very plain to see. The Cloister alphabet is over two picas shorter.

abcdefghijklmnopqrstuvwxyz

abcdefghijklmnopqrstuvwsyz

abcdefghijklmnopqrstuvwxyz

Courtesy of Composing Room of New England.

16. Faces with large x-heights look bigger

Typefaces with large x-heights—that is, the body of the letter is big, and ascenders and descenders are relatively short—appear larger. So if you need to use a small point size to fit in more copy, choose a typeface with a large x-height, such as Times Roman, Trump, Palatino, or Avant Garde. It'll make your text look airier and more inviting.

Newspapers often are good examples of this principle. News type is usually set in a small size, in narrow columns, and printed on relatively inexpensive, rough paper. A well-designed newspaper will use a face with a large x-height so it seems to have a large, easy-to-read body size.

A face with a large x-height, like the Palatino used here, looks bigger, more open.

Simple, yet elegant
The beautifully understated decor of the main hall contributes to an overall feeling of peace. You'll never feel out of place, because the entire inn is a wonderfully successful merger of simple grace and elegant extravagance.

23

17. Use a "thin" face for narrow columns

In selecting a workable typeface for a publication having narrow columns, pick a face that will not result in too many hyphenated lines, or too many ill-fitting lines requiring extreme word- or letterspacing.

A slightly condensed (thin) face such as News Gothic, ITC Garamond Book Condensed, or Times Roman will probably be more legible than a fatter face. With modern photocomposition techniques, it is relatively easy to achieve the same effect by "minusing" or squeezing an appropriate face slightly to provide better fit.

Before making your final type selection have several test columns set and study the results.

If you set text in an 11-pica column, be sure to select a face of the right size and design. Here we see a fine, fat face that doesn't work. Note the extreme word spacing in the eighth text line.

Tigers on a roll

The Tigers won their third consecutive game Friday, defeating the arch rival Falcons 88-79, despite injuries that have plagued the teams all season.

Two of the Tigers' starters have been sidelined with knee injuries for most of the season, but an inexperienced bench has rallied to fill the gap and the team now stands at 7-4.

18. Decide what to emphasize

One of your first tasks usually is to decide which type elements will receive the most emphasis. The copywriter or client probably will work with the designer to decide what's most important in the piece, and the designer will carry out that decision.

Deciding what should be emphasized isn't always easy. Should the company or product name be displayed? If you're designing an ad to build customer awareness of a new product, you may very well want to emphasize the name above everything else. But if you're designing a report to be sent to company shareholders, the company name could be far less important than the fact that profits went up in the last quarter.

Decide what is important, the grabber, the one or two messages that must get through. Then play up those elements.

The designer of this ad used type size and weight to draw attention to the most important thing first—the call for employees. The second most-emphasized item is the company name. Everything else is subordinate to those two pieces of information.

WE NEED EXPERIENCED PEOPLE IMMEDIATELY!

ACCOUNT EXECUTIVE: Consumer and Business to Business. 3-5 years experience required. Salary to 60K.

ART DIRECTOR: Strong Design. Good manager. Production knowledge a must. Salary to 50K.

COPYWRITER: Business to Business. 3-5 years experience required. Salary to 50K.

Send resume and samples if applicable to Ray Maher. Maher/Hartford, Inc., 91-93 Elm Street, Hartford, Connecticut 06106. No calls please.

MAHER
ADVERTISING/PUBLIC RELATIONS

Courtesy of Maher/Hartford, Inc.

19. Display all, display nothing

When you're deciding what elements will receive the most emphasis, remember if you display too many items, you have displayed nothing. Competition between displayed elements can create confusion in the viewer's mind, a visual overload, and the reader blanks out, turns the page.

This ad fails because it tries to emphasize everything—even the addresses vie with the store name and the main slogan for attention.

> # Our Competitive Rates And Quality Service . . .
>
> *—Appraisals*
> *—Repair and cleaning*
> *—Custom-designed jewelry*
>
> ## . . . *Make Us the Choice Of Discriminating Buyers*
>
> *We're so sure you'll love us that we offer a money-back guarantee if you're not completely satisfied.*
>
> *Visit our two locations:*
>
> 2218 N. SYCAMORE   CORNER OF MAIN AND 16TH
>
> # GEMSTONE JEWELERS OF CENTREVILLE
> ## "We take jewels seriously"

20. Use more than size to create emphasis

Using big type is one of the most common ways to create emphasis and it is very effective. In almost any type of printed piece, the reader will read the largest type first.

But size isn't the only means of creating emphasis, and it's not always the right one. The character of the company, the audience to be addressed, the design approach selected—all influence how design elements should be displayed. For example, a jewelry advertisement might call for a light touch that would be destroyed by a screaming headline. Instead, the designer might set the most important items in a relatively small size of a dainty typeface, but call attention to those items by leaving lots of white space around them.

Remember, there are many ways besides size to create emphasis, including using color, a bold typeface, rules, or white space.

21. Match the type size to the project

Type size is directly related to the product, the people addressed, and the company or organization represented. For example, a newspaper advertisement directed to an upscale audience, placed by a leading furniture store, would call for a type treatment far different from the same kind of advertisement prepared by a furniture store going out of business.

Why? Because the fine furniture store has established its position in the marketplace based on a refined, sophisticated image. That image is best conveyed with smaller display type, more white space, well-designed roman faces, and smart, modern design.

A failed furniture store isn't concerned with pride and position in its advertising. All it wants to do is move furniture, to shout at an audience interested in snapping up a bargain. Big, rugged letters, bright colors, fancy borders, probably a full-page ad—that's the path it would follow.

Decisions about type size are also tempered by the design approach. A typeface with the correct character, set in three-inch letters, selling fine wines, could be absolutely right—if teamed with the correct design; mishandled, it could be criminal.

Here the design of the ad, with its tasteful use of white space, draws attention—not large type. Big or bold type would have contradicted the atmosphere of quiet charm conveyed by the wording and the splendid, imaginative logo.

BORN TO NANTUCKET

For generations, a fortunate few have enjoyed the seductive charms of Nantucket—the cobblestone streets, the ocean breeze, the carefree island ambience.

Nashaquisset invites you to share the island way of life. This village of beautifully landscaped traditional homes will soon be taking shape on the outskirts of Nantucket town.

If you have ever dreamt of owning a home on Nantucket, we urge your reply.

Priced from the $200's. To be placed on Nashaquisset's priority preview list, call (617) 864-7250, or write Cambridge Equity Associates, 1130 Massachusetts Avenue, Cambridge, Massachusetts 02138.

Nashaquisset — a village of nantucket

This is not an offering to New York or New Jersey residents or where prohibited by law.

© 1987 Primary Design, Groveland, MA. Art director: Jules Epstein. Designer: Revelle Taillon.

22. Determine the reading distance

Before you decide what size type to use, determine, if you can, what the reading distance will be. Take, for example, type to be used on a poster. If viewers can't get closer than, say, twenty feet, that tells you you've got to select relatively large faces. But sometimes posters are for display in a home, restaurant, or theater lobby, where the reader can get within inches. Obviously, quite small (probably explanatory) type can be used, as well as larger type for main headings.

Type for a 35mm slide, both the type sizes and number of lines, is determined by the size of the hall and the screen size. If the hall seats 5,000 people, the slide should have no more than a few words in large letters if people in the back rows will be able to read what's projected. To be safe, make up some sample slides and project them in a hall the size of the one to be used.

23. Consider custom

Custom helps set parameters on the selection of proper type sizes for certain design projects. Business cards, for example, rarely use a large type size. The same is true of formal announcements and invitations, which are usually 10- or 12-point, perhaps 14-point.

You can break convention successfully, but make sure you know what you're doing. Unless you're going after a special effect, it may be wise to stay within the customary bounds.

The type size you choose can be influenced by what's customary. For instance, formal invitations normally don't use type that is either unusually small or unusually big. By keeping the type size within those parameters but using a sans serif type, this invitation is both traditional and modern.

Hahnemann Hospital
cordially invites you to attend
a private reception in
celebration of
our new
Same Day Surgery Center

please join
our honored guest
Dr. Barbara Rockett
Past President,
Massachusetts Medical Society
on
Tuesday, November 17, 1987

Courtesy of Hahnemann Hospital, Boston.

24. The size of the printed piece helps determine type size

Type size is also directly related to the project size in many cases. If you're preparing a brochure to fit a regular #10 business envelope, it can't be more than 3¾ inches wide when folded. To fit heads within that width, you'll be limited to a range from 14-point through, perhaps, 36-point condensed. Any larger and you won't be able to fit more than a few characters per line. If a head is to extend across all three inside pages, of course, larger sizes of display type can be used.

July 15:
347 Years of European Occupation:
What Hath We Wrought
Kathleen Anderson, Manomet Bird Observatory
Director Emeritus

July 22:
Planting for Wildlife — How you can attract
Wildlife in Your own Backyard
Al Bussewitz, Staff Botanist and Photographer,
Arnold Arboretum

July 29:
Contemporary Issues in Coastal Zone Management
Lori Thayer, Community Planner for Metropolitan Area Planning Council

Field Trip: Migrating Shorebirds at Scituate

Shorebirds have been called "champion migrants," because most fly round-trip distances of 2,000-16,000 miles between their arctic breeding grounds and South American wintering areas each year. Many shorebirds stop along the New England coast between July and October. Some are difficult to identify, all have fascinating life histories, many need conservation assistance.

This field trip, led by expert birder and Marshfield conservation commissioner **Warren Harrington,** is designed to give you basic information about shorebirds. We will go to Third Cliff Beach, Scituate, an area favored by migrating birds. If you'd like to improve your skills in identifying these amazing visitors to our beaches and wetlands, and to learn more about their incredible annual journeys, join us!

Date: Saturday, August 8
Time: 9:00 a.m.
Cost: $8 non-members/$5 members

Pre-registration is necessary. We will send instructions upon receiving your registration form.

Courtesy of Manomet Bird Observatory.

Since this brochure was designed to fit in a standard business envelope, the line measure had to be relatively short and the heads couldn't be too large. The typeface and sizes used here are quite legible and still allow for plenty of white space.

25. Follow Brady's Golden Rule of Spacing: Space together elements that belong together

To avoid all spacing problems in your projects, regardless of the medium, you need learn but one simple rule. The rule applies to *every* situation.

It is, simply put: *Space together those elements that belong together!*

Think about it. It sounds too simple to be true, but it's true nonetheless.

This rule is based on a simple principle I mentioned earlier—that white space combines or links graphic elements. It delivers an important message. Handled appropriately, it can be very useful, but it can be deadly if it misleads the reader.

So space together anything you want the readers to think of as linked elements, and use white space to separate graphic elements that are separate units.

An example of bad use of spacing I saw recently in a magazine advertisement was this: the advertisement carried about eight short paragraphs of text, two or three lines each, set 30 picas wide in 10-point roman, upper and lowercase. No paragraph indentation, just two points of extra space between paragraphs. Result? Visual confusion. It looked like one long paragraph. Another two points of white space would have been perfect for separating the paragraphs, and there was plenty of space available.

Schmidt and Associates,
a consulting agency,
is pleased to announce
it has joined with
Evanson Consultants, Inc.
to provide services through
our network of offices:

Evanson and Evanson
Serving Pennsylvania,
New York, Connecticut

Schmidt-Mason Co.
Serving Ohio,
Indiana, Illinois
Michigan

▲ This smart, with-it design shows perfect spacing of elements. The extra space above each firm's name separates the information about that firm from all the rest.

▶ The spacing between elements in this mail-order catalog is used to create three definite groupings—the descriptive material, the list of contents, and the ordering information.

Our "Showcase" Sampler

Here are five great-tasting treasures from Vermont, in an impressive gift collection. Our "Showcase" Sampler is truly an exciting introduction to the foods we're most famous for, and includes:

- Center Cut Cob Smoked Ham Steak (1 lb.)
- Pure Vermont Maple Syrup (½ pint)
- All-Beef Summer Sausage (10-oz. stick)
- Cob Smoked Breakfast Bacon (¾ lb.)
- Cob Smoked Canadian Bacon (½ lb.)

192-706 The "Showcase Sampler **$31.45**

Courtesy of The Harrington Ham Company.

26. Don't fill up all the white space

Make sure your design allows enough white space around all graphic elements—don't fill every square pica of space.

Why? One reason is that the reader's eye is attracted by white space. If you fill it all up with type, you'll have a much harder time getting the reader's attention.

Another reason is that if you don't have any white space you won't be able to keep design elements separate or show their relationships. Everything will run together in one big blur. For example, you need white space around type within a ruled box so that the box and type form a unit that's set off from the type around it. You also need white space around some ads to assist in fending off competing advertisements in a publication.

Far better too much white space than too little.

In Celebration of Our 15th Anniversary

THE SUNBURST IMPORTING & EXPORTING CO.

INVITES YOU TO AN
O P E N   H O U S E

SUNDAY, OCTOBER 18,
NOON TO 5 P.M.

MONDAY, OCTOBER 19,
NOON TO 5 P.M.

TUESDAY, OCTOBER 20,
4 P.M. TO 8 P.M.

- Exhibition of unusual items from around the world
- Drinks and snacks provided
- Strolling minstrels (Sunday only)
- Chance to win $100 in merchandise

4388 E. JACKSON BLVD.
SUITE 201

This ad leaves almost no white space, creating a cluttered, unattractive look. The reader hardly knows where to begin reading.

The imaginative use of white space in this ad for Prisma Lighting Inc. attracts the reader's eye and creates one single impression, rather than a confusing jumble.

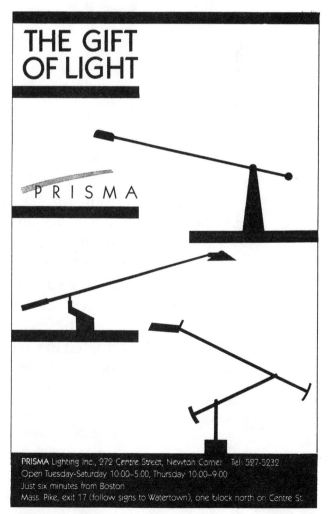

Courtesy of Prisma Lighting Inc.; Janet Theurer, designer.

CHAPTER 2

The Technical Considerations of Design

YOUR CREATIVE DECISIONS about what typefaces and sizes to use and what elements to feature will largely determine how well the printed message comes across. But those decisions can't be put into action until you've made dozens more decisions about the details of design—how long the lines should be, whether text will be ragged or justified, how much space you'll leave around subheads, the leading between lines of text, to name a few.

These decisions are every bit as important as those discussed in Chapter 1. If text lines are too long or the leading is not adequate, the reader's eye will get lost dropping from one line to the next. If you make the wrong decision about word spacing, or kerning, or punctuation marks, you can damage legibility or even stop the reader cold. You might project an amateurish feel that discredits the message you're trying so hard to deliver.

In this chapter I'll show you how to handle some of the most important details of type design—details you'll face every time you work with words to be set in type.

1. Use down-style heads

Today's down-style headings—set flush left with the first line beginning with a capital and all following words lowercase, except for proper names—are clean and crisp. They're much easier to read, minus the visual acrobatics caused by the common practice of capping every major word. It's also much faster to set and to proofread headlines this way . . . and time is money.

More and more, designers are using down-style heads, where only the first word is capitalized. As you can see, down-style heads look cleaner, speed comprehension.

For Just $1.99, You Can Expand Your World Beyond Your Imagination

When you purchase the first of these beautifully illustrated encyclopedias for just $1.99, you'll open doors to realms you never even knew existed.

For just $1.99, you can expand your world beyond your imagination

When you purchase the first of these beautifully illustrated encyclopedias for just $1.99, you'll open doors to realms you never even knew existed.

2. Break heads properly

Each line of a heading must break properly. This is both important and difficult to achieve, since it requires effort and creativity from both the designer and copywriter.

To have the most impact, each line of a head should break on a phrase, by sense. Otherwise, the reader may have a difficult time following the sense of the heading, may emphasize the wrong words, may not pick up the pacing of a catchy phrase.

To be most effective, headlines should be broken by phrase, as shown in the first example. The visual breaks occur where a spoken pause would; notice the unnatural breaks in the second example.

Before you invest
in a computer system
for your new business,
call Thompson's

We deliver first-rate
products right to
your own door

It's the copywriter's or editor's job to count characters and thus write heads that fit properly, and to instruct the designer and typesetter to set them line for line, as typed.

Even though it is primarily the copywriter's job to write display copy that breaks well, there are instances where the designer can help.

When the wording can't be changed—where the display type, for example, is part of a jingle or the rest of the piece is geared toward that one key phrase—the designer can choose a point size that makes the type break properly or redesign the piece to avoid a bad break.

Here's an example of how a designer can help a head that wasn't written to break well. The original newsletter head read like this:

> ERD attaches recycling
> provision to
> waste-to-energy license

This heading fails on all counts. It's hard to tell that the word *recycling* modifies *provision*; the preposition *to* is separated from its object *license*; and the character count is bad. The head, rebroken by phrase, should read:

> ERD attaches
> recycling provision
> to waste-to-energy license

3. Place more white space above a head than below

Here's a very common, thoroughly annoying error illustrated through two examples clipped from a newsletter. Each example gives readers an incorrect signal. Even though the subheads belong with the text lines *below* them, not those above, the amount of white space below the heads separates them from their text. The result: some confusion, a hesitancy, as the reader overcomes the visual misdirection.

A subheading that's correctly spaced has more white space above the heading than below. This signals the reader that the head and following text function as a unit.

If, for mechanical or technical reasons, you can't handle placing more space above the subhead than below, use a full line space above and below or a full line space above and no extra space below.

Minister Pierre DeBane have spread the word, to Europe and beyond, that these slaughtered pups are "adults."

THE FACTS

This confusing rhetoric, widely reported by the press in Canada and the U.S., quite naturally convinced the

Extra space below a heading separates it from the text, rather than pulling the two together.

supporting plant operation. The staff building will also house a new training simulator to be delivered in 1984.

Production

- Completed 184 training courses and classes including safety, proficiency, steam operations, hydro operations,

Using a full line space above and below a subhead is acceptable, but *not* commendable.

Summary of Significant Accounting Policies

Du Pont observes the generally accepted accounting principles described below. These, together with the notes that follow, are an integral part of the consolidated financial statements.

Accounting Changes
In 1985, the company adopted Statement of Financial Accounting Standards No. 87, "Employers' Accounting for Pensions," and No. 88, "Employers' Accounting for Settlements and Curtailments of Defined Benefit Pension Plans and for Termination Benefits," for all U.S. pension plans. In 1986, the company adopted these Standards for its non-U.S. pension plans; the effect was not material.

Basis of Consolidation
The accounts of wholly owned and majority-owned subsidiaries are included in the consolidated financial statements. Investments in affiliates owned 20% or more and corporate joint ventures are accounted for under the equity method. Investments in noncorporate joint ventures in the natural resource areas are consolidated on a pro rata basis. Other securities and investments are carried generally at cost.

Marketable Securities
Marketable securities are carried at cost plus accrued interest, which approximates market value.

Inventories
Substantially all inventories are valued at cost as determined by the last-in, first-out (LIFO) method; in the aggregate, such valuations are not in excess of market. Elements of cost in inventories include raw materials, direct labor, and manufacturing overhead. Stores and supplies are valued at cost or market, whichever is lower; cost is generally determined by the average cost method.

Property, Plant and Equipment
Property, plant and equipment (PP&E) is carried at cost, and, except for petroleum and coal PP&E, is generally classified in depreciable groups and depreciated by an accelerated method that produces results similar to the sum-of-the-years' digits method. Depreciation rates range from 4% to 12% per annum on direct manufacturing facilities and from 2% to 10% per annum on other facilities; in some instances appropriately higher or lower rates are used.

Petroleum and coal PP&E, other than that described below, is depreciated on the straight-line method at various rates calculated to extinguish carrying values over estimated useful lives.

Generally, the gross carrying value of PP&E (including petroleum and coal) surrendered, retired, sold, or otherwise disposed of is charged to accumulated depreciation, depletion and amortization; any salvage or other recovery therefrom is credited to accumulated depreciation, depletion and amortization. Maintenance and repairs are charged to operations; replacements and betterments are capitalized.

Oil and Gas Properties
The company's exploration and production activities are accounted for under the successful efforts method. Costs of acquiring unproved properties are capitalized, and impairment of those properties, which are individually insignificant, is provided for by amortizing the cost

thereof based on past experience or the estimated holding period. Geological, geophysical, and delay rental costs are expensed as incurred. Costs of exploratory dry holes are expensed as the wells are determined to be dry. Costs of productive properties, production and support equipment, and development costs are capitalized and amortized on a unit-of-production basis.

Coal Properties
Costs of undeveloped properties and development costs applicable to the opening of new coal mines are capitalized and amortized on a unit-of-production basis. Costs of additional mine facilities required to maintain production after a mine reaches the production stage, generally referred to as "receding face costs," are expensed as incurred; however, costs of additional air shafts and new portals are capitalized and amortized.

Intangible Assets
Identifiable intangible assets, such as purchased patents and trademarks, are amortized on a straight-line basis over their estimated useful lives. Goodwill is amortized over periods up to 40 years on the straight-line method.

Income Taxes
Provision for income taxes is based on pretax financial accounting income, which differs from taxable income because certain elements of income and expense are reflected in different time periods for financial accounting purposes and tax purposes. On a cumulative basis, such timing differences result in a net excess of pretax financial accounting income over taxable income; deferred income taxes on this excess have been provided for in the financial statements using the gross change method. Under this method, reversing timing differences are reflected at historical tax rates.

Investment tax credits have been included in income in the period earned (the flow-through method).

Provision has been made for income taxes on unremitted earnings of subsidiaries and affiliates, except in cases where these earnings are permanently invested or the resulting income taxes would not be material.

Foreign Currency Translation
The company has determined that the U.S. dollar is the "functional currency" of its worldwide foreign operations. Foreign currency asset and liability amounts are translated into U.S. dollars at end-of-period exchange rates except for inventories, prepaid expenses, and property, plant and equipment, which are translated at historical rates. Income and expenses are translated at average exchange rates in effect during the year except for expenses related to balance sheet amounts that are translated at historical exchange rates. Exchange gains and losses are insignificant in amount and are included in income in the period in which they occur.

Reclassifications
Certain reclassifications of prior years' data have been made to conform to 1986 classifications.

31

Used with the permission of the Du Pont Company, External Affairs Department, Room D-8120, Wilmington, DE.

This well-designed annual report
from Du Pont shows excellent
spacing around subheads.

4. Use more leading for sans serif or bold type

Leading (pronounced "ledding") is the printer's term for the amount of space between lines of text. It gets its name from the metal blanks, or leads, printers once used to separate lines of type. Text can be set solid—with no extra space between lines—although one or two points of extra spacing are normal.

Bold or sans serif type may require slightly more leading than roman text to enhance legibility. In addition bold type sometimes needs extra leading to lighten its color or weight.

Text set in sans serif type is more likely to suffer from "doubling," where the reader's eye doesn't drop to the next line of text, but instead doubles back to the same line; proper leading prevents this.

Sans serif and bold typefaces often require more line spacing than roman types do. Here, the Times Roman type at top looks fine on a 10-point leading, but the Serif Gothic and Century Bold types could benefit from an extra point of leading.

To be a good manager, you must trust and respect your employees. You must be available to them if they have problems, but you must trust them to do their jobs when they don't. You should assume that they are trying to do their best and change that assumption only when you have direct evidence to the contrary.

To be a good manager, you must trust and respect your employees. You must be available to them if they have problems, but you must trust them to do their jobs when they don't. You should assume that they are trying to do their best and change that assumption only when you have direct evidence to the contrary.

To be a good manager, you must trust and respect your employees. You must be available to them if they have problems, but you must trust them to do their jobs when they don't. You should assume that they are trying to do their best and change that assumption only when you have direct evidence to the contrary.

5. Faces with long descenders need less leading

Certain of the older typefaces, such as Garamond, Bembo, and Caslon, are designed with long descenders and may require little or no extra space between lines. In effect, the leading has been built in by the designer. On the other hand, a text face with short descenders may require extra space.

If in doubt about how much leading you need, set samples or get your typographer's advice. Some typefaces can be composed with either short or long descenders.

6. Increase leading to lighten weight

In Chapter 1, I wrote about the weight or color of a type mass. This critical factor can be altered by increasing line spacing. A page that is too dark can be lightened by adding leading. Two points of leading between lines of 10-point type is the addition of 20 percent white space, which dilutes the color of the type mass.

7. Adjust spacing after typesetting

There are times when you must adjust spacing so that the reader is not misled. A small example? When the last line of a paragraph is short, it can create what appears to be extra white space above the next subheading. By eliminating some or all of this extra space, you make all the subheadings *appear* to have the same spacing. It's creative "cheating."

Here's an example of creative cheating. The line above the first heading is short and would have left too much space above the heading. But a minor adjustment prevented that. Even though there is less space between the lines of text above and below the first head, the visual effect is one of equal spacing.

Unlike other home equity loans, the Bank of Boston Home Equity Credit Line gives you three ways to pay, including one where you can pay interest-only for up to five years. And, you get a line of credit and payback term for as long as you own your home.

We Pay Your Closing Costs

If you're a Bank of Boston deposit customer on the day you close the loan, we'll pay all closing costs*–a savings of $290-$400. All you need is a checking, savings, NOW or First Rate account, a certificate of deposit or a Deposit IRA at Bank of Boston.

Save Even More on Interest

If you maintain combined deposit balances of $5,000 or more at Bank of Boston beginning on the day you close, we'll pay your closing costs* and reduce the Annual Percentage Rate (APR) on your Home Equity Credit Line–from our Base Rate** plus 2% (currently 9.5% APR) down to our Base Rate plus 1.5% (currently 9.0% APR) and if you maintain $25,000 or more we'll reduce your rate even further to our Base Rate plus 1% (currently 8.5% APR). APR may vary.

All owner-occupied, one-to-four family homes and condominiums in Massachusetts are eligible for a credit line anywhere from $10,000 to $100,000 or more. Your particular amount may be up to 75% of the current value of your home, minus the existing first mortgage balance.

Get full details today. Call toll-free 1-800-851-LOAN, send in the coupon, or stop at any of our offices. But hurry, this offer ends March 31, 1987.

8. Forget the alphabet-and-a-half rule

A hoary, ink-stained rule of thumb says a line of type should not be any longer than an alphabet and a half in the same point size (some say two alphabets). That rule is meant to keep designers from setting type in blocks that are too wide—if the lines are too long, the reader's eye can get lost.

But the rule is far too simplistic. If you use it to determine the line length for 12-point Garamond #248, for example, it allows a line only 19 picas wide. Yet one of my type specimen books shows a sample block of 12-point Garamond set 24 picas wide and it is perfectly satisfactory, highly legible.

One key reason the alphabet-and-a-half rule doesn't always work is that it doesn't take into consideration line spacing. Extra line spacing can eliminate doubling because it helps direct the eye as it moves from one line to the next. So instead of blindly following the alphabet-and-a-half rule, consider type size, x-height, line spacing, the overall legibility of the typeface, ink color, and the type of paper (text or coated).

Even though this sample of 12-point Garamond #248 breaks the alphabet-and-a-half rule, it's perfectly easy to read.

> HE took his ship away. The affair was not discussed at home, though each of us gave it some private despondency. We followed him silently, apprehensively, through the reports in the *Shipping Gazette*. He made point after

Courtesy of Composing Room of New England.

9. Increase line spacing as you increase line length

If you want to increase the line length of a block of text, you may also have to increase the line spacing. By adding a bit more white space between each line, you'll make sure the reader's eye doesn't go astray as it drops from line to line.

But beware: too much leading and your type page or display paragraph falls apart and readability is damaged.

As you increase line lengths, be sure to also increase line spacing, but not so much that your text begins to fall apart. The first sample is 11-point Times Roman on a 12-pica line. It's quite readable with 12 points of leading. The same type on a 22-pica line, though, looks better with 13 points of leading.

> First fill out requisition form 1-B, indicating the quantity needed, expense account number and delivery date. Then sign the form and keep the yellow copy for your records. Send the white copy to the fulfillment department and the blue copy to your supervisor. If you have not received a confirmation notice in ten days, call extension 3441 and request verbal confirmation.

> First fill out requisition form 1-B, indicating the quantity needed, expense account number and delivery date. Then sign the form and keep the yellow copy for your records. Send the white copy to the fulfillment department and the blue copy to your supervisor. If you have not received a confirmation notice in ten days, call extension 3441 and request verbal confirmation.

10. Never use hyphens in display type set ragged right

If you are setting a book, magazine, or brochure and all the text will be set ragged right (with an uneven right edge), your typesetter will usually set each line as full as possible, using hyphens where necessary. That's okay.

But if you're setting just a few paragraphs for display or design purposes, the lines should have no hyphenation. It's simply not needed!

Also, make sure the lines do not form a pattern or shape, as shown here. All line endings must be truly ragged. Use fixed, not variable word spacing—it provides an even color and enhances both legibility and the overall appearance of the type.

▼ The text in this advertisement shows correct setting of ragged right copy—the lines don't form any particular shape, but are truly ragged.

Why we'd rather be a turtle.

While other companies
are bragging about
their speedy
service,
we'd like to
let you know that
we don't think faster
is necessarily
better.
We take more
time with each
of our customers,
giving you the
attention and
respect you
deserve.
So if you want
to be treated like
more than just a deadline,
look for a turtle,
not a hare.

▲ Don't allow ragged copy to form shapes like the zigzag in this advertisement. Line endings should be random, or the effect can be distracting.

The stars above.
The city below.
And heaven
in between.

The lofty atrium. The sunken living room. The intimate dining salon. The gourmet kitchen. The three balconies — each with incredible views of Boston. The library. The luxurious jacuzzi in the master bath. The private roof deck with hot tub where you can bathe in sunlight, enjoy a dazzling display of city lights below, or stand in a shower of stars spilled from a bowl of up-turned midnight sky.

Experience the Empire Suite. The $1,000,000 penthouse at The Grand. ($850,000 unfurnished.)

Call 731-5570.

The Grand is a Parencorp Development.

THE
GRAND
Brookline, MA

Courtesy of The Grand.

11. Don't run headings the full column width

News headings should be written so that the longest lines fill about seven-eighths of the column width, not the full column width. Otherwise, when two heads of the same type size appear next to each other, the reader tends to read across the narrow column space between heads, reading the two heads as one unit.

If your heading has more than one line, make the line endings ragged, rather than having all lines the same length.

News headings should always be ragged right with some lines less than the full column width, like these headlines from an award-winning daily.

Area

Salary request rejected by advisory board

FOXBORO — The advisory committee has rejected a request from the board of health to transfer $1,500 to pay former plumbing inspector Tom Eisenhauer.

Eisenhauer was hired to inspect septic systems on a per-hour basis until a new health agent is hired. The board is asking that he also

Norton hopes for state aid on new library

(Continued from Page 1)
Norton Library Director Jay Scherma is optimistic that Norton will get some aid.

"There's not a whole lot of money, but they have assured us that the Norton library is a likely candidate for some of it," Scherma said.

40

12. Avoid tight word spacing

Word spacing is important: It affects the color of the text block, and too much or too little can affect legibility.

For generations compositors have been taught that text material should have, as a minimum, a space equal to a third of an em between words, although spacing can be adjusted for certain letter combinations. (One great strength of hand composition, it should be noted here, is the ability of the trained compositor to vary word spacing throughout the line, while machine composition provides equal space between all words in a line.)

Some graphic designers now argue that the thickness of the lowercase *i* should be used to establish correct word spacing. They maintain that such tight spacing improves legibility, speeds reading, and improves comprehension, particularly for sans serif text.

Such tight word spacing should be used with caution. It may look fine as seen on a mechanical or proof, but consider the visual handicaps that can occur when type is printed on glossy stock (glare) or rough text paper, then add the variations in press inking from gray to heavy black, and tight spacing may well create visual problems for many readers.

Since the earliest days, standard word spacing for lowercase type has been a third of an em. Here's one fine example using standard spacing.

Join us in the service of America's grandest warship...

Old Ironsides!

From foc'sle to quarterdeck, forestay to capstan, the *USS Constitution* is little different in 1986 than when she was launched in 1797.

For nearly 200 years, our nation has so revered this majestic fighting ship and her history-shaping exploits that she has remained in commission with the U.S. Navy to this day.

As the warship that tamed the infamous Barbary Pirates and, on several occasions, bloodied the nose of the justly proud British navy, Old Ironsides is the floating embodiment of the bold spirit with which our nation defended its interests and independence during its early years.

Much of the heritage we so value today was forged upon her broad, sweeping decks—the same decks that echoed to the footfalls of the U.S. naval heroes of the likes of Stephen Decatur, Isaac Hull, William Bainbridge, and Edward Preble.

As a member of the USS Constitution Museum, you will be part of a non-profit institution especially chartered for the purpose of assuring a continuing national appreciation of Old Ironsides.

Over the years, more than 50 million visitors from all over the nation and throughout the world have come to see for themselves this legendary warship. It is in giving these visitors a meaningful understanding of her weapons, implements, fittings, rigging and construction—as well as her epic role in history—that the

Fund-raising brochure and text written and typeset for the USS Constitution Museum by Yankee Publishing.

13. Visually space all-cap lines

No all-cap line should be considered properly composed unless it is spaced by hand and by eye. The reason is simple: Certain letters require more or less space between them to look proper. For example, the letters *M* and *N* require additional spacing when they fall together, while other letters, such as *L* and *A*, show more space than needed.

For word spacing, a line of capitals should use an en space as standard, adjusted, of course, for certain letter combinations.

DINING

©1987 by The New York Times Company. Reprinted by permission.

Visual spacing is imperative for all-cap lines. The eye is comfortable with the word *Dining* because the D has been tucked under the adjoining i and the two n's and the two l's have been given a whisker of space to separate their serifs. *Fresh Bluefish Tales* needs additional word spacing, though. Eliminating the useless period would have allowed more space.

FRESH BLUEFISH TALES.

14. Don't letterspace text

Letterspacing text—adding extra space between the letters—changes the color and kills the grace of the typeface. One bad, but fairly common example: space added between every letter of the last word or two to fill out a short line. It is a practice deplored by purists. Goudy is quoted as saying something like, "People who letterspace lowercase type would sleep with pigs."

It is considered less gross to letterspace an entire text line, rather than a word or two, but in either case it is not recommended as it usually interferes with the reading process.

You can, however, letterspace type in heads to lengthen the line and create a stronger heading. The effect in this example is not unpleasant. But note the extra space placed between the two words, as it should be. Also note that the rule underline has been selected with care, so its thickness is slightly less than that of the letterforms and it harmonizes perfectly with them.

Avoid letterspacing text like this—it is distracting and hard to read.

Kerry also snagged the chairmanship of the International Economic Policy, Oceans and Environment subcommittee. That gives him some influence on ocean treaties that are important to Massachusetts, an entrance to acid rain problems on an international scale and the ability to work on foreign industrial and economic competition. Again, it follows the Kerry agenda.

Letterspacing can strengthen headings. Note the special touches that make the *Cross Currents* heading work—the extra space placed between the two words and the use of an underline that is slightly less thick than the letterforms.

CROSS CURRENTS

15. Use kerning to improve fit

To *kern* is to fit individual letterforms together to eliminate unnecessary and unsightly spacing created by certain combinations of letters. For example, when set in a large type, the letters *T* and *o* often need to be kerned so that the *o* slides partway under the top stroke of the *T*.

You definitely want the blessings of kerning, but not the unsightly kerning too often seen, where characters touch one another. Your goal is enhanced legibility, not visual static that impedes comprehension.

Note: Do not confuse *kerning* with the term *proportional spacing*, which simply means that all letters in the typeface in question appear on the proper width bodies. In other words, a cap *M* is designed so that it takes up more space than a narrower letter, such as *I* or *J*.

Proper kerning would have helped this head greatly. The spacing between the letters FAC and WAT is poor and the letters I and N overlap.

FACES TO WATCH IN '88

16. Squeeze some typefaces

Squeezing or *minusing* type means uniformly reducing the space between letters. As opposed to kerning, where spacing is altered on a case-by-case basis, squeezing type reduces the space between all letters throughout a block of text.

Some typefaces, particularly those designed with more white space between letterforms than is always needed, look better "minused" than they do set regular. Trump is a good example. When minused, the letters have a better overall relationship and the resulting composition is more legible. Ask your typesetter for examples of minused settings. Some type specimen books show minused blocks of text type as well.

But be careful. Type minused more than necessary can suffer a loss of legibility. You should be sensitive to both problems. Be sure to examine samples and judge for yourself.

Trump is a typeface that can be successfully squeezed or minused.

Some typefaces, particularly those designed with more white space between letterforms than is always needed, look better "minused" than they do set regular. Trump is a good example. When minused, the letters have a better overall relationship and the resulting composition is more legible. Ask your typesetter for examples of minused settings. Some type specimen books show minused blocks of text type as well.

17. Use swash letters sparingly

Many of the fine old faces, such as Garamond and Caslon, have swash (ornate) letters in addition to the regular letters. If you are designing a newsletter heading such as the one shown here, utilizing swash characters appropriately and sparingly certainly can be effective in conveying character. This organization maintains Boston's Old State House, built in 1713, so the swash letters create a neat, dignified newsletter heading that's completely in keeping with the character of the society.

But don't overdo swash letters. They can be distracting and hard to read when too many are used together, and can lose their impact. And make sure their old-fashioned appearance is in keeping with your message.

Swash letters can easily be overdone, as in *Yuletide,* but can create a dignified look when used properly, as the Caslon italic caps do in the newsletter heading for The Bostonian Society.

YULETIDE

THE BOSTONIAN SOCIETY

Used by permission of The Bostonian Society/Old State House.

18. Use old-style figures with care

Old-style figures provide a nice touch and you should make use of them, but only in an appropriate project, such as an advertisement for colonial style furniture or the program for a classical music concert.

The use of old-style figures in this heading adds a touch of class. Old-style figures can help you avoid the rigidity of lining figures, but only with an appropriate design like this one.

KEENE STATE COLLEGE
Arts Center on Brickyard Pond
1987-88 season

Reprinted with permission from the Arts Center on Brickyard Pond, Keene State College; Chris Nerlinger, designer.

19. For easy typeface identification, look for g, y, a, e, or *t*

Even the expert can be stumped, so don't feel bad if you have difficulty naming Times Roman at a glance. The trick is to look for a letterform with unusual character, such as a lowercase *g* (or *y, a, e, t*). Then check the particular letter against similar faces in a type specimen book.

Other distinctive elements can also help you identify a face. For example, Goudy loved the diamond-shaped period and dot over the lowercase *i*, and created letterforms, such as *O*'s, with thick elements on a slant.

g
Melior

ɢ
Piegnot Medium

g
Windsor

Process lettering from Typographic House Inc., Boston.

Identifying the typeface used in a particular piece can be tough. Look for distinctive letters or characteristics. The lowercase *g*'s of Melior, Peignot Medium, and Windsor illustrate the great difference between faces. The line of Goudy Bold #294 shows some of the special characteristics that distinguish it from other faces.

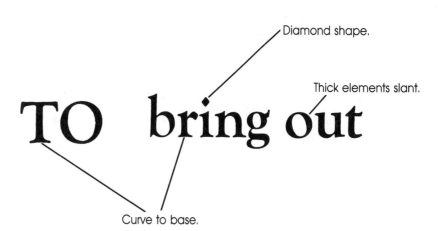

Diamond shape.

Thick elements slant.

TO bring out

Curve to base.

20. Don't be fooled when you measure a typeface

When you measure a typeface from the top of an ascending letter to the bottom of a descending letter, the result in points is not necessarily the type size. A 24-point letter might well measure 20 points. The only way to be absolutely sure of the size is to compare with samples in a type book.

Each lowercase letter *h* shown here is a 24-point character—honest!

h **h** h **h** h **h** h **h** **h** h

Excerpt from 13th edition of *Pocket Pal,* used with permission of International Paper Company.

21. Don't create your own small caps

You cannot combine 14-point capitals with 10-point capitals to make your own 14-point caps and small caps. The letters and words become "hot" to the eye, calling attention to themselves. Small capitals *must* be created by the typographer when the capitals are designed so that they will relate properly.

And here's a fact few people capitalize on: Small capitals are often more beautiful than their capitals.

MORE THAN WORDS CAN CONVEY

Intrigued? For more information call 339-8929

Forest Park

Mansfield, MA □ *Marketed by Park Realty* □ *Homes Priced from $440,000*

Reprinted by permission of The Broderick Corporation.

Using caps and small caps can be very effective. Note the two very different uses in the realty ad and in the list of Goudy types.

A LIST OF GOUDY TYPES
By date; for alphabetical list, see Page 282

Year	Design No.		Page No.
1896	1	CAMELOT	37
1897	2	UNNAMED	39
1897	3	A "DISPLAY" ROMAN	41
1898	4	DEVINNE ROMAN	44
1902	5	PABST ROMAN	52
1903	6	PABST ITALIC	54
1903	7	POWELL	55
1903	8	VILLAGE	57
1904	9	CUSHING ITALIC	61
1904	10	BOSTON NEWS LETTER	62
1904	11	ENGRAVERS' ROMAN	63
1905	12	COPPERPLATE GOTHICS	64
1905	13	CAXTON INITIALS	65
1905	14	GLOBE GOTHIC BOLD	66
1905	15	CASLON REVISED	67
1908	16	MONOTYPE NO. 38-E	70
1908	17	MONOTYPE NO. 38-E ITALIC	70
1910	18	NORMAN CAPITALS	75
1911	19	KENNERLEY OLD STYLE	77
1911	19A	KENNERLEY OPEN CAPS	81
1911	20	FORUM TITLE	82
1912	21	SHERMAN	85
1912	22	GOUDY LANSTON	86
1914	23	GOUDY ROMAN	89
1914	24	KLAXON	91
1915	25	GOUDY OLD STYLE	92
1915	26	GOUDY OLD STYLE ITALIC	95
1916	27	GOUDY CURSIVE	97
1916	28	BOOKLET OLD STYLE	98

278

Reprinted by special permission of the publisher from Frederic W. Goudy, *Goudy's Type Designs,* The Myriade Press, Inc., Second Edition, 1978.

22. Check spacing around the em dash

If the em dash is so wide it touches letters on one side or the other (depending on the adjoining letters), it's a poorly designed character. A well-designed em dash for text use has a built-in shoulder on each side to prevent the bar from touching adjoining letters.

When an em dash touches the letters, the effect is distracting, annoying. If necessary, the compositor should insert a thin space to prevent the dash from touching another character.

This example of Goudy Old Style shows a properly designed em dash. Notice the built-in shoulders that keep it from touching the adjoining letters.

> Net income in this department is up 6 percent—as compared to an increase of just 1.3 percent last year—and is expected to show significant growth again next quarter.

23. Set punctuation the same as the word it follows

When a comma, colon, or period follows a word set in italic or boldface, the punctuation mark must also be in bold or italic. Even if the majority of the text is set in roman, the punctuation should match the word it follows. The exceptions to this rule are quotation marks, exclamation points, question marks, parentheses and brackets. They should be set in keeping with the type style of the rest of the sentence.

24. Treat an ellipsis like a word

The ellipsis is grand and useful and is almost always set incorrectly. It *must* be treated as a word and have word spaces before and between each period, like this . . . and not like this ... and especially not like this...which is pretty terrible.

The ellipsis is a useful punctuation mark loved by writers and much too often misused by typesetters. It should have word spaces before and between each period—none of these do.

...AND BRIEFLY

dollar a retiree ... can save is very important. All we're asking

"form of a safety-sheath. . .ex the name of its deviser, a colonel in the Guards."

25. Use ampersands only in proper names

Don't use the ampersand (&) in text matter, dialogue, or headings. It is not a proper substitute for the word *and*. The ampersand is used correctly only in the names of those firms or products that use the symbol.

The letters *et* (Latin for *and*) create an ampersand, as Goudy beautifully shows here.

26. Be careful with proper name prefixes

If you're setting in caps a proper name with a prefix—DeAngelis, MacDonald, LeFavour, or some such—you properly set it one of two ways: DE ANGELIS (all caps and a thin space between the prefix and name) or LeFAVOUR (with only the first letter of the prefix capped, the remaining letters either in small caps or lowercase, and no space). Never set it as DEANGELIS.

Nothing stops the eye faster than a name like MCHENNESSY. It's a sure set-up for a double-take. Either use a lowercase *c* or put a thin space between the prefix and the rest of the name.

JOHN PATRICK NORMAN MCHENNESSY—THE BOY WHO WAS ALWAYS LATE
John Burningham. Crown, $12.95
ISBN 0-517-56805-5
Every morning, John Patrick Norman McHennessy sets off along the road to learn and is waylaid by very unusual occurrences—a lion in the woods, a crocodile in the river, a tidal wave—that, according to his teacher, simply *couldn't* have happened. So, every afternoon he must stay after school to write out his punishment. But one

PATRICIA MCGOVERN

Patricia McGovern, chairman of the Senate Ways and Means Committee. While not a member of the business community, her work on behalf of universal health-care legislation has the potential for affecting most businesses in the commonwealth.

27. Leave space between bullets and text

When type bullets are used to set off items in paragraphs, don't mash them against the text. Use a thin space to give the bullet enough room to do its job.

Bullets come in many sizes and weights, and it's easy to select one that may be too powerful for its intended use. Err on the side of moderation, but avoid weakness.

When type bullets are used to set off items use a thin space to give the bullet some air. Also, select bullets of the proper "weight." The top example is bad, the bottom excellent.

To determine whether the gain or loss on the sale of an asset is capital gain or loss or ordinary gain or loss, you must classify the assets sold as:
●Capital assets;
●Real property and depreciable property used in your business and held for more than 6 months; and
●Other property—for example, stock-in-trade, inventory, or property used in your business and held 6 months or less.

Brainerd says these essential steps help form a successful coalition:
• Get all the concerned players together. They must cooperate and agree on a goal.
• Clearly identify which issues the coalition will address.
• Establish a game plan for addressing these issues which must include a means for broad-based dissemination of information.
• Establish effective communication methods for educating the public. It is important that the coalition speaks with a unified voice.
• Hire a coordinator. Like George

©1986, Journal of American Insurance.

CHAPTER 3

Special Design Elements

ALMOST EVERY DESIGN PROJECT contains a few challenges—elements that are slightly different from anything you've handled. It might be complicated tabular material, or a set-in initial that has a quotation mark before it, or a bit of verse that needs to be displayed properly.

This chapter is devoted to those special elements. It'll give you rules for handling two of the most common of these problems—tables and set-in initial caps—as well as guidelines for a few other tough type problems.

1. For tables, choose a face with uniformly sized figures

You probably haven't thought about it, but the figures that come with a particular typeface may be very important if you are going to set tabular matter. All figures must have the same body width or they will not align vertically when set in columns. Old-style figures, for example, often are not uniformly sized.

While some well-designed text faces offer you a choice of figures, they don't all have figures that align. So be sure to make this important check before selecting a face for tabular work.

Be careful when choosing typefaces to be used in charts. Some have figures that don't line up well. This chart is set in Antique Olive Bold Condensed, which has figures that do not align. The Figure 1 is on a smaller body than other numbers.

	Results of September poll		
	For	Against	Percent For
Democrats	10,111	6,717	60.0
Republicans	3,989	4,929	44.0
Independent	110	140	44.0

2. Align column headings at the bottom

A very common error is to align stacked column headings at the top word. It is much better to align all such heads at the bottom. Bottom alignment is neat and clean, and aids readership because it reduces eye travel.

You may either center column headings or align them right or left, your choice.

▶ Column headings in a chart like this should align on the bottom word, not the top. This example shows how aligning on the top creates awkward white space below the shorter headings.

Comparison of Local Delivery Services					
Company	Night Pickup	Weekend Pickup	Large Parcel Handling	Rush Service	Insurance
SpeedEZ	Yes	Yes	No	No	Yes
Pronto	Yes	Yes	Yes	Yes	Yes
D'Angelo	Yes	No	Yes	Yes	No

▼ Aligning column heads along the bottom word, as in this chart from Du Pont's annual report, gives a clean, neat look that's easier to follow.

1986	Biomedical Products	Industrial and Consumer Products	Fibers	Polymer Products	Agricultural and Industrial Chemicals	Petroleum Exploration and Production	Petroleum Refining, Marketing and Transportation	Coal
Sales to Unaffiliated Customers [1]	$1,150	$2,839	$4,786	$3,657	$3,396	$1,926	$7,893 [2]	$1,501
Transfers Between Segments	5	81	63	158	538	902	318	38
Total	$1,155	$2,920	$4,849	$3,815	$3,934	$2,828	$8,211	$1,539
Operating Profit	$ 123	$ 297	$ 946	$ 471	$ 347	$ 389	$ 623	$ 189
Provision for Income Taxes	(32)	(100)	(447)	(207)	(128)	(448)	(227)	(59)
Equity in Earnings of Affiliates	(3)	(28)	43	2	22	—	18	—
After-Tax Operating Income	$ 88 [3]	$ 169 [4]	$ 542 [5]	$ 266	$ 241 [6]	$ (59) [7]	$ 414 [8]	$ 130

Used with the permission of the Du Pont Company, External Affairs Department, Room D-8120, Wilmington, DE.

3. Repeat column headings

If a table breaks and runs onto more than one page, you *must* repeat the column headings. Don't expect the reader to remember what each column is, or to flip from page to page to find out.

If at all possible, you should also incorporate references to indicate what units are being used both in the heading and with the first entry in the column. In other words, use the dollar sign or percent sign in the heading *and* with the first line of the column beneath it. If the table runs over to a second page or more, be sure to carry over these references.

4. Keep columns close together

Reduce the space between columns of figures to make charts easier to read. Quite likely the reader's eye will get lost as it travels from the state name to the sales figure in this chart.

When you plan tables with columns of figures or words, place the columns as close together as possible, not spread out to fill the page's width. The most difficult task for the reader of a table is to read from one column to another without getting lost. Anything to reduce eye travel between columns will help.

SALES BY STATE, YEAR TO DATE

State	Sales
Alabama	$15,468
Arizona	9,300
Arkansas	23,650
California	90,562

5. Avoid leaders

Leaders are the rows of dots designed to lead the eye from one column in a table to another. But there is nothing beautiful about a line of leaders. In fact they're ugly, so avoid them when you can.

For example, many times the design of a table of contents can eliminate leaders. How? One way is to simply set the words flush left, followed by a comma (or space), then the page number. Thus:

7. When leaders really lead, 107.

Easy, neat, cost saving.

If you must use leaders, opt for open leaders (ones with more space between dots), preferably aligned from top to bottom.

Figure 1. Assets, Liabilities, and Surplus For Medical Malpractice JUAs
(Dollars in Thousands) as of February 1985 (Latest Figures Available)

State	Statement Date	Assets	Liabilities	Surplus
Florida	6/84	50,569	60,585	–10,016
Kansas	6/84	6,013	6,013	–0–
Maine*	12/83	6,204	3,843	2,361
Massachusetts	12/83	240,429	549,416	–308,987
New Hampshire	12/83	12,101	44,231	–32,130
New Jersey*	12/83	79,764	127,854	–48,090
New York	12/83	254,194	503,187	–248,993
Ohio*	9/83	30,535	8,261	22,274
Pennsylvania	12/83	40,883	32,654	8,229
Rhode Island	12/83	44,750	85,925	–41,175
South Carolina	12/83	17,144	30,042	–12,898
Tennessee*	12/83	19,402	26	19,376
Texas	12/83	48,574	32,949	15,625
Wisconsin	12/83	67,487	72,758	–5,271

*Deactivated — No Longer Writing Business

Source: JUA Annual Reports and/or Annual Statements as compiled by The Alliance of American Insurers.

©1986, Journal of American Insurance.

Table of Contents

From *Smithsonian,* February 1985.

With good, imaginative design you can avoid the use of unsightly leaders. Here are two fine examples. The chart from the *Journal of American Insurance* uses rules to direct the eye, while the *Smithsonian* table of contents places the number so close to the article title that nothing at all is needed to lead the eye.

6. Use only top and bottom rules for tables

Stay away from full-rule boxes for tables. They are old-fashioned and unnecessary. They also cost money, since the rules either have to be set or laid in on the mechanical. Also, type within the box has to be set to a shorter measure.

Use rules only at the top and bottom to create an "open" box. It's a far better technique. Or use a screened background to create your box. Just make sure you use the correct weight of screen. Too dark a screen will make the table hard to read.

Open boxes like this one are far more appealing and more modern than a full box with rules on all four sides. Open boxes are also easier to create, quicker to change.

Is the Service You Now Receive Better, Worse, or About the Same as You Would Expect?

	1983 %	1987 %	Change in % Points
Better	28	23	-5
Worse	23	20	-3
About the Same	47	55	+8
Don't Know	2	2	0
Total	100	100	

7. Use initial letters to create impact

Initial letters—large or decorative letters used at the beginning of text sections—provide many opportunities for creative designers to develop powerful, dramatic, and pleasing graphic attention grabbers. They may be stand-up (the initial letter sticks up above the text), cut-in (the first few lines of text are indented to accommodate the initial letter), or used totally on their own.

This cursive capital *H* makes a dramatic statement. Perfectly balanced, the weight of its thick and thin elements, its positioning, blend beautifully with the strong italic used for the rest of the heading.

Haute couture is a fashion never-never land in which made-to-order clothes cost thousands. But it has considerable creative impact on less rarified areas.

©1987 by The New York Times Company. Reprinted by permission.

8. Use text caps for the first few words following an initial letter

All the world is using set-in initial letters, usually incorrectly. If you're going to use them, learn the typographic rules. Then you can break them, if you wish, with full awareness.

Rule No. 1 is this: When using an initial letter, the rest of the first text word *must* be set in text capitals. Otherwise, the strong initial overpowers the text letters.

If the first word is short (like *The* or *An*) set the next word or two in caps, too. Always have a minimum of six or eight cap letters following the initial.

The first initial *W* seems to outweigh the text that follows it. Notice how much more balanced the second example looks with the first few words set in small caps.

Whenthe late violinist Bronislaw Huberman founded the Palestine Orchestra in 1936, staffing it with Jewish musicians who were fleeing from Nazi persecution, he little knew that one day it would be

Jane and Michael Stern West Redding, Connecticut

They feel that they wear the mantle of crusaders for the simple foods that everyone loves, a cause supported both by their writing and by all of the "champion square meals" that they cook and serve at home. **by Edie Clark**

When friends come for dinner at Jane and Michael Stern's, they are likely to be served tuna casserole and Coca-Cola cake. "Those are my two favorite corny dishes to serve to guests," Jane says. "We don't always say what they are, especially the cake. If we don't tell them it's made with Coca-Cola, they think it's some exotic chocolate recipe." Inside this menu is a statement, a philosophy.

Jane and Michael Stern have become iconoclasts in an overstuffed food world,

Courtesy of *Yankee Magazine*.

9. Align initial letter and text at top and bottom

The top of the initial letter *must* align with the top of the *ascending* letters in the first text line. The base of the initial cap must align with the *baseline* of the last text line opposite it.

This means you must select your text face and its line spacing with care, making sure your initial letter is the correct size. It's easy enough today to enlarge or reduce initials a hair to insure a perfect fit.

This is an excellent example of how the initial letter should line up with the text. The initial letter aligns with the top of the first line of text and the base of the last line of text.

VARIATIONS in spelling, legitimate or otherwise, are only one of the inscrutable problems computers face in dealing with free-form text. A more broad-reaching problem they encounter is that of distinguishing the appropriate textual content. The piezoelectric properties of the material used in, say, an antistatic device for the record indus-

©1987 by The New York Times Company. Reprinted by permission.

10. Set text lines to fit properly around initial letter

The first text line following an initial letter *must* butt snugly against the initial. This provides a clean top line and leads the reader's eye into the text smoothly. The spacing is especially important if the initial is a cap *A,* for example.

Here's the rule for insuring that the balance of your text lines fit properly: Leave as much space *next* to the initial as the space *between* its base and the ascenders of the text line below.

When an initial letter is separated from the text by two picas, as in this illustration, you can readily understand the importance of making sure the first text line butts snugly against the initial. See how much more smoothly the text reads in the second example.

At nine institutions around the country this month 108 patients with progressive kidney disase are starting a new therapy involving controlled, low-protein diets. If the clinical trials uphold doctors' hopes, the therapy could delay or even replace the need for kidney dialysis among many of the more than 70,000 patients whose kidneys work with less than 10 percent efficiency.

KATHARINE HEPBURN IS THE ONLY movie star I know who lives right around the corner from me. It's a brownstone house on East 49th Street in Manhattan, and sometimes her chauffeur is sitting outside in the car, waiting to take her shopping or up to Connecticut, where she has a country place. A few years ago, we had a big snowstorm, and a neighbor reported that Miss Hepburn, who was then about 75 years old, was out shoveling the sidewalk and the stoop.

"Miss Hepburn, why are *you* shoveling the snow?" he demanded.

"Because it's on the ground," the great lady sensibly replied and went right on shoveling.

Reprinted with permission from *Parade,* ©1987.

11. Don't omit the quotation mark

When a quotation mark precedes an initial letter, many people simply leave it out. But you shouldn't omit punctuation for design reasons, and quotation marks can be incorporated easily.

You have three choices for handling a quotation mark. You can set it in the same type and size as the initial letter, you can set it smaller than the initial letter, or you can use quotes the size of the text type.

If the initial cap is large and set in a heavy Gothic face, for instance, the quotation mark can be big and ugly, so you may opt to set it in the same face but a couple of sizes smaller. The smaller quotation mark will alert the reader to the fact that the material is quoted without calling unseemly attention to itself.

Quotation marks don't have to interfere with the initial letter. The use of smaller opening quotation marks would certainly have improved the first example, as you can see by comparing it to the second example. The quotes and the initial are in complete harmony there. Even double quotation marks can be handled gracefully, as shown by the third example.

"**L**ast year was a bear-market year. And when you do well in a bear-market year, as we did, I think you have to end up pretty well satisfied."
    Roy Millenson is talking about his last year as watcher of federal funding

"**U**NCLE TOM'S CABIN" was out of print by the late 19th century. But today, 50 years after publication, "Gone With the Wind" still sells about 250,000 copies a year in the United States and 100,000 around the world. In virtually every one of those years, more than 40,000 *hardback* copies were sold. By 1983 there were at least 185 editions in print, and 25 million

Copyright © 1987 by The New York Times Company. Reprinted by permission.

" '**T**ake care of the sense and the sounds will take care of themselves,' " the Duchess tells Lewis Carroll's Alice. It might seem reasonable advice, even if it weren't meant more as a play on the British proverb "Take care of the pence and the pounds will take care of themselves." It's not, I must say, a motto I follow. *Nothing* in a book, from the wording of the ded-

From "Sound and Sense" by Paul Fleischman in *The Horn Book Magazine,* September 1986, p. 551.
Reprinted by permission of The Horn Book, Inc.

12. Use superior figures for footnotes

Nothing will mark you as a beginner more quickly than using multiple asterisks to indicate footnotes. The practice apparently came about because many personal computers had few characters available for use as reference marks.

With most typefaces, you can use the standard reference marks—the asterisk, dagger, double dagger, degree sign, paragraph mark, etc.

But you can run short of such characters. Your best choice might be to use superior figures, small numbers set slightly above the text like this[2] to indicate footnotes. If you use superior figures in the text, use regular size figures for the footnote itself.

13. Align Roman numerals on the right

Although almost universally miscomposed, despite one simple rule governing their use, Roman numerals are a neat typographic element.

The rule? Always align Roman numerals on the right, *never* on the left. You can use periods following each numeral, or omit them—your choice. That's all you need to know.

Always look for the longest Roman numeral before determining your line length. Then set the line with the longest numeral first, for guidance.

The table of contents from the book *The History of Painting in America* shows roman numerals used properly—aligned on the right, not the left.

From *The History of Printing in America*, by Isaiah Thomas.

14. Use hang quotes in verse

If you set a single line of verse, or a stanza or quotation, consider using hang quotes. Let the opening quotation mark hang out into the left margin and align the second type line on the first text letter. Used carefully in the right place, a hanging quote is a real grace note.

Using hang quotes may seem like a typographic trifle, but what a powerful one!

*"Freedom of
the press
belongs to
those who
own one."*
—*A. J. Liebling*

15. Figures and sans serif type don't always mix

If you are setting text in which chemical formulas will appear, be careful with sans serif faces. In some, the lowercase letter *l* and figure *1* as well as the cap *I* are so much alike you can't tell them apart. In text, that's usually no problem; in chemical formulas they can be a major headache.

Some typefaces have i's, I's, and 1's that look similar, as does Vogue Lite, shown here.

abcdefghijklmnopqrstuvwxyz 1234567890
ABCDEFGHIJKLMNOPQRSTUVWXYZ

Courtesy of Wrightson Typographers, Boston, Massachusetts.

16. Consider all-cap faces for special uses

Some typefaces are designed with capitals only, no lower case. Two such beautiful faces are Hadriano and Forum. No problem, as long as you realize there is no companion lower case.

If you are designing a certificate or diploma, either Forum or Hadriano is an ideal face incorporating the needed character. (The figures, incidentally, are old-style, as they should be, in keeping with the Roman forebears of the faces.) Since certificates traditionally are rather formal and deliberately old-fashioned, the lack of lowercase letters doesn't create a problem.

Hadriano is a cutting by Goudy that comes in caps only.

NOW IF THE

Courtesy of Composing Room of New England.

PART TWO

PRODUCTION AND PRINTING

TYPESETTING, PASTE-UP, AND PRINTING transform the graphic design into reality. But too often the looseness, freedom, and flair created by a graphic designer when preparing a comprehensive layout, or even a pencil rough, seem to disappear when type is set and mechanicals are prepared. The artistic succumbs to the rigidity of type, the discipline of fixed margins, the coldness of ruled lines. It is a change, a shock, a metamorphosis people new to graphic arts must become used to—and learn to overcome as far as possible. The trick at this point is to make sure that the final printed piece will show—to the greatest degree possible—all the spontaneity and creativeness of the original layout.

How do you retain the creative verve of the layouts? You do it by making sure that typesetters, illustrators, paste-up people, and printers all receive explicit instructions on what you want. You are the quality control expert, and you can accept bad work at high prices, or insist upon good work at no higher prices.

The designer is always the key person in assuring that the finished product is correctly produced, meets all predetermined specifications, and fulfills, within the limitations of the printing process, the expectations of the customer.

Establish your standards up front. Accept only top quality typesetting, and insist that you see galleys for proofing before board work is started. Make sure all type set incorrectly (as well as all typographical errors) will be corrected at the typesetter's expense.

Before the mechanicals are released for printing, go over all special camera, platemaking, and finishing instructions with the printer. In this way all production problems can be anticipated and the printer has no excuse for not producing and delivering the finished product exactly as agreed upon.

In like manner, designers should propose both paper and ink colors in conference with the client, who should always retain veto and approval power. Paper costs too much to rush into a decision before all possible choices have been explored, keeping both cost and appropriateness firmly in mind.

The finest design, the best possible typography, the most expert printing can all come to grief if cooperation and communication fail at any point in the creative and production cycle. The next three chapters will help assure such disasters don't happen to you.

Working with Typesetters and Paste-up Artists

TECHNOLOGICAL CHANGE takes place rapidly today—in typesetting equipment and methods, in presses, in bindery techniques. Working in graphic arts is like living in the eye of the hurricane. Every day is a learning experience.

But there are some basics, some verities, that never change (although they can be adapted by the truly knowledgeable). This chapter deals with some of those basics. It provides tips and techniques for working with graphic arts specialists to make both your life and theirs more productive, to enhance communication, to reduce or eliminate errors as far as possible.

The material is not complex. It's the kind of common sense information you'll use forever to deal with a world that is continually in a state of flux.

1. Prepare clean copy

It shouldn't have to be said, but your copy should be clean and easy to read. Clean copy cuts down on the number of errors and cuts typesetting costs. Ask typesetters for their pet horror stories about dirty or illegible copy.

Type all copy double- or triple-space. Indent all paragraphs at least eight spaces so the typesetter doesn't have to guess where paragraphs begin. Write corrections, additions, and all special instructions in clear, readable handwriting. Use copyediting symbols to mark changes.

Typesetters routinely charge extra for composing "bad" copy—material with many corrections, additions, and deletions—all items that slow keyboarding. Your manuscript should be as clean as possible, with corrections made neatly and legibly.

Chapter 4, p. 4

1. Prepare clean copy

It shouldn't have to be said, but your copy should be clean and easy to read. Clean copy cuts down on the number of errors and cuts typesetting costs. Ask typesetters for their pet horror stories about dirty or illegible copy.

Type all copy double or triple space. Indent all paragraphs at least eight spaces so the typesetter doesn't have to guess where the next paragraphs begins. Write corrections, additions, and all special instructions in clear, readable handwriting. Use copy editing symbols to mark changes.

2. Don't make typesetters guess

Don't assume knowledge on the part of typesetters and mark-up people (the typeshop specialists who translate your instructions into specific shop instructions. You must mark your copy so that you receive exactly what you want. If a block of type is to be set ragged right, for example, mark it so the typesetter will understand exactly what you want 1/m-deep rags with no hyphens or more gentle rags using hyphens, for example. Another case in point: When you give specs for text, don't forget to indicate how wide the paragraph indent should be.

3. Mark overall specifications on page one

Any type specifications that apply throughout the manuscript should be indicated on the first manuscript page. These specifications, which usually cover the basic text and headings, should be written clearly and simply, in a form similar to this:

2. Don't make typesetters guess

Don't assume knowledge on the part of typesetters and mark-up people (the typeshop specialists who translate your instructions into specific shop instructions). You *must* mark your copy so that you receive exactly what you want. If a block of type is to be set ragged right, for example, mark it so the typesetter will understand exactly what you want—deep rags with no hyphens or more gentle rags using hyphens, for example. Another case in point: When you give specs for text, don't forget to indicate how wide the paragraph indent should be.

3. Mark overall specifications on page one

Any type specifications that apply throughout the manuscript should be indicated on the first manuscript page. These specifications, which usually cover the basic text and headings, should be written clearly and simply, in a form similar to this:

Text: 10/12 Times Roman × 18 pi, just. ¶ indents 1 em

That means you want 10-point Times Roman type with 12 points leading from baseline to baseline, set 18 picas wide and justified (with right and left edges even); paragraph indents are to be one em.

Overall specifications should be marked on a separate spec sheet or on the front page of a manuscript, as shown here. To learn the language of the mark-up people, note how the directions are followed—or missed—when you proof your galleys.

Text: 9/10 Palatino x 22 pi, justified.
Paragraphs indent 2 pi.
A: 24 pt. Helvetica Bold, V & lc, F/L.
26 pts b/b above, 14 pts b/b below.
B. 10 pt. Helvetica, U + lc, F/L
18 pts b/b above, 12 pts b/b below.

Partnerships, Adams, p. 1

(A) Partnerships

A partnership is the relationship between two or more persons who join together to carry on a trade or business with each person contributing money, property, labor, or skill, and each expecting to share in the profits and losses of the business.

(B) Husband-wife partnerships

If you and your spouse carry on a business together and expect to share in the profits and losses, you may be partners regardless of whether you have a formal partnership agreement. If so, you should report your income or loss on Form 1065, U.S. Partnership Return of Income, and also include your respective shares of the partnership net income or loss on separate Schedules SE (Form 1040), Computation of Social Security Self-Employment Tax.

(b) Partnership profits

(and other income and gains) are not taxed to

must be stated

4. Mark complicated type specs in the copy

Any specifications that can't be explained in one or two lines up front should be marked where they're needed within the copy. This is particularly true for complicated items such as tables, but can also apply to some headings and special elements such as bulleted lists.

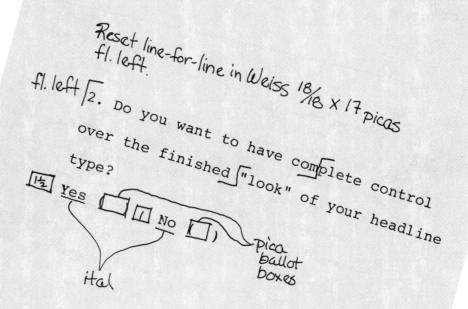

Complicated or special bits of typography within a job should be marked on the page where they occur.

5. Measure line spacing from baseline to baseline

Line spacing (or leading) is measured from baseline to baseline. That means if your text type is 12-point, with two points of leading, the measurement in points from the base of one line of type to the base of the next line will be 14 points.

Baseline measurement is the commonly accepted standard for photocomposition. It is the only practical method because of the extreme flexibility of line spacing—you can specify line spacing in fractions of points!—and the wide variation in type size possible with phototypesetting equipment.

Indicate the correct line spacing by marking the amount of space in points from the base of one line of type to the base of the next line. You can use the abbreviation "b/b" or "b to b."

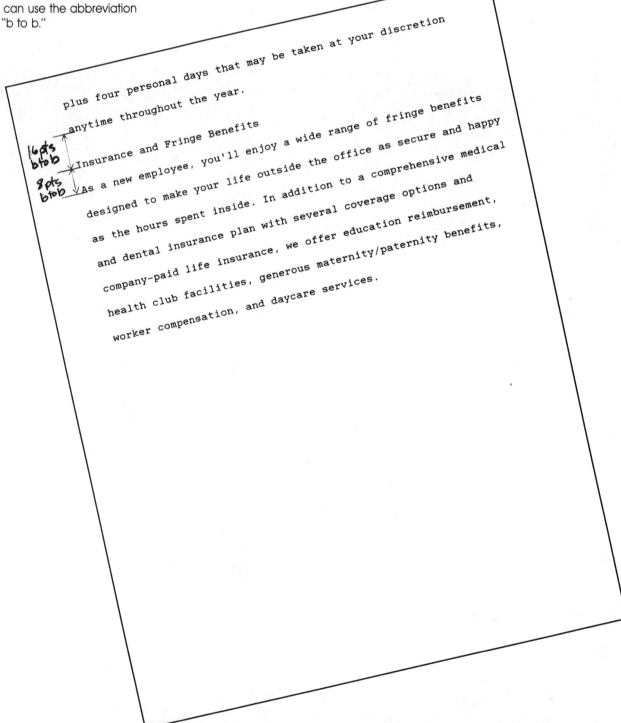

6. Always keep the layout with the manuscript

The layout should always travel with the manuscript because it can answer many typesetting questions that arise—sometimes in the middle of the night. Also, each display line to be photocomposed to fit a particular space or size should have a tissue rendering so the compositor knows exactly what is required.

7. Like the tango, it takes two to proofread

Proofreading accuracy really requires the use of two people: A proofreader and a copyholder who reads aloud so the proofreader can concentrate on the proof. Solo proofreading is a sure invitation to missed errors, caused by eyes constantly jumping from proof to copy and back.

If you need more than one set of galleys, be sure the typesetter knows this at the time the job starts through the shop. Mark one set as your master and consolidate all corrections and author's additions on this set. Retain another marked set for yourself so you can answer any questions that come up. Galleys cost money, so order no more than you really need.

8. If you must proofread alone, trick your eyes

If you absolutely can't use two people to proofread, your biggest challenge will be to keep from reading what *should* be there instead of what really is. These two tricks will help:

● If the copy isn't long, try reading each line of type backwards, one word at a time. That'll keep you from falling into normal reading habits, and you'll look at each word as a word, not part of a sentence.

● Place an index card or piece of paper beneath the line of type you're reading, moving it down one line at a time as you progress through the proof. This helps isolate the type being read so that mistakes can be seen more easily.

9. Learn proofreaders' marks, and use them

Any good dictionary will have a listing of proofreaders' marks. Try the *American Heritage Dictionary, 2nd College Edition*, page 992, for an excellent presentation. It not only shows the marks, but also exactly how to place them in the margin of the proof *and* within the proof.

It's important to note your corrections within the text and in the margin. Typeset material usually doesn't provide enough room in the copy itself to make corrections, so the mark within the proof indicates where the correction goes and the marks in the margin give necessary details about the correction. For example, when you cross out a word and realize too late you shouldn't have, simply place a row of dots under the word crossed out and write "stet" in the margin. Both marks mean "let it stand."

The governor rejected the state attorney general's report, saying that the advisory committee did not have access to all the facts and "was biased in a certain direction." He refused to quote specific instances where the report was faulty, but said he would appoint his own committee to look into the problem.

A spokesperson for the attorney general's office called the report "accurate and balanced" and said the formation of a new committee will only delay much-needed reforms. "The governor is responding to political pressures," the aide said. "He's the one who is biased, not this report."

The attorney general could not be reached for comment.

Leaders in both houses of the state legislature urged the governor and attorney general to resolve their differences on this issue. Democratic leaders maintain that the governor is trying to create an issue that Republic candidates can use to their advantage in the fall election, but Republican officials deny that there is any political motive behind the delay.

"This is a serious matter that cannot be decided lightly," one high-ranking Republican said. "I don't think anyone should be criticized for trying to make sure that all the pertinent information has been gathered, and that is has been gathered by an impartial body."

The corrections on this galley have been marked correctly by the proofreader.

PROOFREADERS' MARKS

Instruction	Mark in Margin	Mark in Type	Corrected Type
Delete	ℰ	the ~~good~~ word	the word
Insert indicated material	good	the word	the good word
Let it stand	stet	the ~~good~~ word	the good word
Make capital	cap	the word	the Word
Make lower case	lc	The Word	the Word
Set in small capitals	SC	See word.	See WORD.
Set in italic type	ital	The word is word.	The word is *word*.
Set in roman type	rom	the *word*	the word
Set in boldface type	bf	the entry word	the entry **word**
Set in lightface type	lf	the entry **word**	the entry word
Transpose	tr	the word/good	the good word
Close up space	⌒	the wo rd	the word
Delete and close up space	⌒	the woord	the word
Spell out	sp	2 words	two words
Insert: space	#	the word	the word
period	⊙	This is the word	This is the word.
comma	⌃	words words, words	words, words, words
hyphen	^=^/^=^	word for word test	word-for-word test
colon	⊙	The following words	The following words:
semicolon	⌃;	Scan the words skim the words.	Scan the words; skim the words.
apostrophe	⌄	Johns words	John's words
quotation marks	⌄/⌄/	the word word	the word "word"
parentheses	(/)/	The word word is in parentheses.	The word (word) is in parentheses.
brackets	[/]/	He read from the Word the Bible.	He read from the Word [the Bible].
en dash	1/N	1964 1972	1964–1972
em dash	1/M / 1/M /	The dictionary how often it is needed belongs in every home.	The dictionary—how often it is needed— belongs in every home.
superior type	⌄	$2 = 4$	$2^2 = 4$
inferior type	⌃	HO	H_2O
asterisk	⌄	word	word*
dagger	†	a word	a word†
double dagger	‡	words and words	words and words‡
section symbol	§	Book Reviews	§Book Reviews
virgule	/	either or	either/or
Start paragraph	¶	"Where is it?" "It's on the shelf."	"Where is it?" "It's on the shelf."
Run in	run in	The entry word is printed in boldface. The pronunciation follows.	The entry word is printed in boldface. The pronunciation follows.
Turn right side up	⊃	the word	the word
Move left	⊏	⊏ the word	the word
Move right	⊐	the word	the word
Move up	⊓	the word	the word
Move down	⊔	the word	the word
Align	‖	the word the word the word	the word the word the word
Straighten line	=	the word	the word
Wrong font	wf	the word	the word
Broken type	×	the word	the word

Copyright © 1985 by Houghton Mifflin Company. Reprinted by permission from THE AMERICAN HERITAGE DICTIONARY, SECOND COLLEGE EDITION.

Here's some of the shorthand printers have devised and used for many years to indicate typographical errors. Learn these symbols and use them.

10. Use nonreproducible blue ink

When proofreading a finished mechanical or any piece of camera-ready copy, make any marks within the printing area with a blue marker the camera cannot "see." These special markers are sold in art shops, and some light blue pencils are okay.

11. Don't allow more than three hyphens in a row

When you finish reading a galley, pause long enough to run your eye down the ends of the lines. Never accept more than three adjacent lines of text ending with hyphens. Never allow a hyphenated word to be hyphenated a second time. Insist on resetting the type (or changing the copy).

This procedure also gives you the chance to check for improper hyphenation. Computer typesetting equipment "remembers" the correct division for many words, but sometimes doesn't have a large enough dictionary for everything. Mentally check the division of all words; go to the dictionary if in doubt.

Using more than three hyphens in a row is visually distracting and makes the text hard to read.

> me to live in Maine but I'm not from Maine," says Susan Kenney, who was born in New Jersey. "It's quiet and comparatively unstressful here. Imagine, life without parking meters!

12. Turn the page around to catch rivers

Text can develop "rivers," where the space between words in several text lines forms a noticeable white channel. Newspaper, magazine, and book publishers usually ignore them, and rightly, since their tight deadlines and tremendous quantities of composed type make resetting impractical.

But if you're setting type for advertisements, for example, and a river occurs, have the lines reset to keep them from spoiling the beauty of the piece. I once had the pleasure of examining a copy of the King James Bible set in England by the Monotype process in which all the rivers had been eliminated by hand respacing. It was magnificent, even though such resetting would today be considered exceedingly impractical.

You can easily find rivers by turning the type proof or page around, so the top of the page faces you, then hold the page at a slant with the bottom of the page lower than the top. Try it. The rivers will jump right out.

A river occurs when word spaces line up vertically, as shown here. When composing specialized items such as advertisements, eliminate rivers by respacing the type.

> My greatest good fortune was that I didn't know that I was doing everything wrong; if I'd done a single thing right, I probably would have failed. If I'd known how hard—statistically speaking—it is to get a first novel published, I might have given up and done what my wife told me to do—sold some more insurance. What suc-cess really means, I think, is looking failure in the face and tossing the dice anyway. You may be the only person who ever knows how the dice come up, but in that knowledge you have something that millions of people will never have—because they were afraid to try. ■

13. Squint at proofs to find hot spots

By squinting at type proofs you can pick up hot spots created by super-tight fittings. Reset spots where letters are so stuffed together that legibility is compromised—any time one letterform distorts another, for example. One recent extreme example: A single sans serif quotation mark stacked over a period ending a sentence. It took a second glance to be sure it wasn't an exclamation mark (!).

This is an unfortunate bit of kerning snipped from an advertisement. It creates a "hot spot" that catches the eye, interferes with reading.

SHOULD.

14. Check hyphens and dashes

The hyphen, en dash, and em dash are commonly misused in typesetting. Make sure:

● The hyphen is *not* substituted for the en dash. This is one error found in much text composition today. (I believe it's the result of long use of the typewriter, where the hyphen must double for the en dash.) The en dash, which is *half* the length of the em dash, is correctly used to represent *to* between figures: the years 1862–1868.

● The em dash doesn't fall at the beginning of a line of text. The em dash is a signal and must be on the same line as the word *before* it to deliver its signal properly to the reader.

Here's one common mistake: This menu uses hyphens rather than en dashes to indicate the word *to.* Neither the hyphen nor the em dash is a proper substitute.

The Eatery

Take-Out Menu

Available Weekdays: 11:30 AM - 2:00 PM and 5 PM - 11 PM
Sundays: 4:00 PM - 9 PM

Appetizers

Chicken Fingers 2.25
Potato Skins 2.50
Vegetable Platter 1.75

Sandwiches

Grilled Cheese 3.25
 w/bacon 3.75
Bacon, Lettuce & Tomato 3.95
Reuben 4.75

15. Check all dates and figures

Figures that have been set incorrectly often are difficult to catch, and even the manuscript may be wrong. So when you encounter the day of the month and a date, check the calendar to make sure that date falls on the day given. Check telephone numbers against the telephone directory whenever possible. Spot-check the addition when you have figures or tables that give totals.

16. Immediately check cross-references

When the reader is referred to material appearing elsewhere on the page or on another page, stop reading and immediately check to make sure the reference is correct. Often these references can't be added until the pagination is determined, so they may not have been checked by the author and editor.

17. Use an experienced paste-up artist

The paste-up artist (board person) can make or break any job. Sloppy board work, exposed rubber or wax left uncleaned, less than rigid adherence to all margin and spacing specifications, a lack of knowledge concerning basic paste-up rules, a skimpy knowledge of printing procedures—all can lead to mechanicals that can create expensive production problems.

18. Give the paste-up artist specific instructions

Make sure all layouts give complete and specific instructions for paste-up. This includes how wide the margins should be, how much space should be left between columns, placement of special items such as photo credits, page numbers, and running heads, length and weight (in points) of any rules to be added during paste-up.

19. Mechanicals need a tissue overlay and cover sheet

All mechanicals should be completed with a tissue overlay on which are written all special camera, platemaking, and finishing instructions. They also need a cover sheet of 65-pound cover stock, clearly marked to identify the job and particular mechanical. This is important. Usually you will store mechanicals for future use, and a sturdy cover will protect them.

20. Vertical type must read from the bottom up

When placing picture credits or any other type lines vertically on the page, the type *must* read from the bottom of the page to the top.

If a whole page is to be printed sideways, the head goes to the left, regardless of whether it is a right- or left-hand page.

Vertical type should read from the bottom up, as shown in the first example, not from the top down, as in the second.

SCOTT ROBINSON

Photo by Paul Alexander

CHAPTER 5

Improving Reproduction

THE BEST OF DESIGNS, the finest selection of typefaces to present character and enhance the message being delivered . . . all can be lost if you choose the wrong paper or ink color, either because the paper and ink don't work together or because one or both destroy the character of your project.

Good taste and judgment are paramount, of course, and they come with experience. To help you as you gain experience, this chapter presents some sound, time-tested advice on handling both ink and paper, and even more importantly, ink and paper in combination.

1. Reduce typewritten mechanicals 5 to 10 percent

In case of emergency—say you must insert a short news story on page one of your publication and there's no time to get type set—you may have to use a typewriter or computer printer. You can produce very usable type by using a carbon-ribbon typewriter or letter-quality printer, cleaning the type element, selecting a well-designed face (not italic or anything fancy), and keeping the print dark.

To improve the quality and sharpen the text, reduce typewritten or computer printout type by 5 to 10 percent. If you prepare the mechanicals 5 or 10 percent oversize with the reduction in mind, your printer can make the reduction when the page negatives are made, at no extra cost. Use 12-point type rather than your usual 10-point and slightly heavier rules than you would normally use.

```
After competing developers talked for
years about building a shopping mall in
the area, the Davis Square Mall in Benson
emerged as the victor in 1988.
    The day before Christmas, a contractor
for mall developer Southwest Development
of South Norway took out a building per-
mit to install foundations for the mall,
and started work this week at the 37.4-
acre site on Robers Avenue and Interstate
487.
    Construction is expected to be in full
gear by spring.  Although two or more of
the six department stores could be open
for business by the 1989 Christmas season,
the major part of the 140-store, three-
```

Reducing typewritten or dot-matrix copy can improve its appearance. This copy was reduced 10 percent.

```
After competing developers talked for
years about building a shopping mall in
the area, the Davis Square Mall in Benson
emerged as the victor in 1988.
    The day before Christmas, a contractor
for mall developer Southwest Development
of South Norway took out a building per-
mit to install foundations for the mall,
and started work this week at the 37.4-
acre site on Robers Avenue and Interstate
487.
    Construction is expected to be in full
gear by spring.  Although two or more of
the six department stores could be open
for business by the 1989 Christmas season,
the major part of the 140-store, three-
```

2. Avoid printing type on top of strong or busy backgrounds

TV programs do it all the time. They roll the credits against a sky full of wind-tossed branches, or attempt to show white letters against the background of a white building—you've seen it many times. That's overprinting.

Overprinting can be done, but often shouldn't be—especially if the photograph or other background is busy, such as the branches, or too strong, like a company logo underprinted in such giant size on stationery it interferes with the typed message.

Overprinting will work only if a strong contrast between type and background is maintained.

Be very careful when overprinting type on top of a busy photograph or graphic. Large or bold type can work well, but smaller or lighter letters may be lost.

3. Be careful when reversing typefaces with thin elements

Graphic designers often wish to reverse a typeface (create white letters on a black background) for visual impact. But care should be taken with certain typefaces. The success of a reverse with Bodoni, for example, with its extreme thick and thin elements, depends on the skill and attention of those operating the offset camera and press. With care, even Bodoni can be reversed beautifully without the thin elements breaking down. This is also true for delicate faces such as Typo Script, Park Avenue, Lombardic Initials, Commercial Script, and many others.

Be especially careful when reversing type in a small point size, since the thin elements will be even more susceptible to breaking down.

Among the many, many typefaces that reverse well are Century Schoolbook, Bauhaus Medium, and Caledonia.

Reversing type can be tricky. The type in the first example is kerned too tightly, creating a blurred appearance; the second sample uses type with thin elements that filled in during printing.

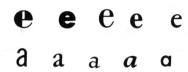

Courtesy of Composing Room of New England.

Always consider the size of the counters (or open spaces) when ordering a reverse. They can vary tremendously between typefaces, as seen here. Bold faces such as the second *e* tend to have small counters that make reverses more difficult. Note the small counter on the fifth *e*, as well.

Faces with small counters, like the Helvetica Black used for the restaurant names here, can plug up in printing, creating a dark, inky effect.

4. Faces with large x-heights and open counters reproduce better

A typeface with a small body size (x-height) is more apt to trap ink in the openings (called "counters") of letters, such as the lowercase *e* or *a*. The technical term is *plugging* or *trapping*.

Letters with shorter ascenders and descenders have larger bodies and provide relatively "open" counters, thus helping to avoid plugging and enhancing legibility.

Lewiston Area

Riverview Inn Dine by the riverside in a truly cozy setting. You can choose from a wide selection of home-baked breads, fresh soup or stew, crisp salads, entrees like lamb and roast beef, and an exquisitely tempting dessert tray. Reservations recommended. MC, VISA and DC. 4:30–9 p.m. Monday through Saturday; noon–8 p.m. Sunday.

The Sidewalk Cafe A charming cafe restaurant with a casual, friendly atmosphere. The menu features American and international cuisine, with dinners ranging from $7.95 to $15.95. Lunch 11 a.m.–2 p.m. Monday through Saturday; dinner 5 p.m–10 p.m. Monday through Saturday; brunch 11 a.m.–4 p.m. Sunday.

5. Coated paper can help when reversing type

When reversing type, your choice of paper can be of key importance. A reverse that will work on coated stock might fail on a textured stock.

6. Screen a head to tone it down

If a typeset head is too big and dominates more than it should, a quick cure is to screen the heading enough to weaken it.

The same technique can be used for rules, line drawings—in fact, for almost any object that has too much muscle and needs to be weakened.

You have a wide range of possible screen effects at your command, ranging from those with very coarse dots to very fine.

7. Use screens to create drama

Screening also allows you to use illustrations imaginatively. Using a fine screen to underprint an illustration, perhaps in color, can be an effective way to spice up a page of type. (Be careful to maintain proper contrast!) A giant letter or figure, properly screened, can be both dramatic and powerful. Likewise, the use of an enlarged screen, perhaps by blowing up a section of a halftone illustration, is an effective technique with its dramatic, bold dot size.

For employers who really want to make a splash with health promotion, Occupational Health has developed a Worksite Health Fair, during which nurses from Norwood Hospital conduct a variety of screening tests, answer questions and give out educational material. "It's a great way to kick off a health promotion campaign in the workplace," said Patty. "It really gets employees thinking about their health."

In the year that Norwood Hospital's Department of Occupational Health has offered health promotion programs to local businesses, their client list has grown steadily. One satisfied client is the Faxon Company of Westwood, Patty's first customer. According

Bag lectures every six weeks or so, and they're always popular.

"I would definitely recommend these health promotion programs to other businesses," she continued. "It's been our experience at Faxon that employees who are healthier and fitter are more productive."

For more information on the health promotion programs offered by the Neponset Valley Health System, call the Norwood Hospital Department of Occupational Health at 769-4000, ext. 2032.

From *Health Pulse*, Summer, 1987. ©The Neponset Valley Health System, Norwood, Mass.

Using screens to create special effects like these can be very dramatic. Make sure the screens are light enough so that type can be easily read.

SESSION 2:

TIPS FOR THE TRAVELLER TO JAPAN

Japan holds in store a vast treasure of fascinating attractions for the tourist. This presentation will introduce famous and lesser known sites for the traveller, as well as helpful advice on such topics as transportation, food, accommodations, and festivals. DR. WILLIAM R. FARRELL, Professor of Management at the Naval War College in Newport, has spent six years in Japan and travels there frequently.

SESSION 3:

ZEN AND JAPANESE AESTHETICS

DR. YURIKO SAITO took her Ph.D. at the University of Wisconsin and is presently Associate Professor of Philosophy at RISD. Her presentation will examine the relationship between Zen Buddhism and Japanese aesthetic sensibilities, with particular emphasis on gardens, architecture and graphic arts.

SESSION 4:

HAIKU AND TANKA POETRY/THE JAPANESE TEA CEREMONY

In part one of this session, DR. MEERA VISWANATHAN, Assistant Professor of Comparative Literature at Brown, will trace the evolution of traditional Japanese poetry, specifically the verse forms *Haiku* and *Tanka (Waka)*. The second hour features a discussion and presentation of *cha-no-yu*, the traditional Tea Ceremony, which has been practiced for centuries in Japan as a spiritual ritual, social occasion and art form. ALLAN PALMER studied the art of tea for 12 years at the Urasenke Society in Kyoto and has adapted presentations of the ceremony for Western audiences in this country.

SESSION 5:

JAPANESE CUSTOMS AND BEHAVIOR/THE EDUCATIONAL SYSTEM OF JAPAN

Tourists and professionals sometimes feel awkward and insecure about the rules of acceptable behavior and etiquette in family, business, and social settings in Japan. DR. WILLIAM BEEMAN, Professor of Anthropology at Brown, has written widely about Japanese society and will share with participants his insights in this area. Part two of the session will feature an assessment of the Japanese educational system, its strengths and shortcomings and the role of schooling in the country's phenomenal economic success. DR. MAURICE GLICKSMAN is Provost of Brown University and has spent several years in Japan as director of a corporate science laboratory.

SESSION 6:

JAPANESE CLASSICAL MUSIC/TRADITIONAL THEATRE IN JAPAN

This two-part session will introduce participants to the unique forms and instrumentalization of Japanese classical music, as well as the traditional dramatic forms (*kabuki*, *no*, and *bunraku*) and their impact on Western playwrights. DR. JANICE KLEEMAN earned the Ph.D. in Ethnomusicology at Berkeley and teaches courses in classical music of Asia in the Music Department at Brown. DR. JOHN EMIGH is an Associate Professor in Brown's Theatre, Speech and Dance Department and received his Ph.D. at Tulane University.

SESSIONS 7 AND 8:

LANGUAGE

For the individual with no knowledge of Japanese, the final two sessions will be devoted to useful phrases for common, everyday situations. Students will learn the sounds of Japanese, the units of currency, the numbers, simple expressions for addressing people, for ordering a meal, a hotel room, train tickets, etc. Suggestions will also be given for useful phrase books and tapes. HIROKO SHIKASHIO is a native of Japan where she graduated from Japan Christian College. In this country she earned an additional degree from California State College in Los Angeles.

▶**Providence:** Thursdays, 7:00–9:00 pm, 8 sessions, October 8–December 3 (no class on November 26) Tuition: **$145** (all 8 sessions); **$108** (sessions 1–6 only) (Note: Tuition will be waived for those members of the Japan-America Society of Rhode Island with family-level memberships or above; the $5 registration fee – payable once a semester – is required. To register, these members should call the Society's Executive Director, Maureen Mezei, at (401) 272-7790.)

From the *Brown University Learning Community's* Fall 1987 catalog.

8. Avoid covering areas with ink

Whether printed in color or black ink, a large solid area can mean grief. If you're using a light paper stock, the ink might bleed through or show through so that type on the verso (the back of the page) is hard to read. Or a solid area can require so much ink that adjoining print receives too much ink.

Large solids also have a bad habit of picking up "hickeys." These bits of dirt can spoil many sheets of paper before the press operator can spot them and stop the press to clean away the dirt.

On a small press, the large solid area can show a mark where the press rollers reverse their travel. To eliminate the problem, the printer might have to shift the job to a larger and more expensive press.

The best remedy is to avoid large solids in your designs if at all possible or, failing that, screen the solid so it'll use less ink.

9. When using screens, steer clear of the "red menace"

You have decided to print your project in red ink, a nice flaming color sure to attract attention. No problem, unless there are screened areas in the job. Then the nice, bright red can become a sickly, repulsive pink.

So be very careful when you screen red. Select one with a fair share of black built in, for the darker reds will usually screen very nicely.

10. Use a recognized color system

When you use words like *red, yellow, brown,* and *green,* you are saying very little. Never tell a printer you want brown ink or red ink, for example; that's too vague.

Take a look at a Pantone Matching System (PMS) or Toyo color manual. The number of red shades in one small color manual on my desk totals eighty-five. That takes you from the orange end of the scale through the browns and on through warm red, rubine red, and rhodamine red, tending toward the violet end of the scale.

Always use a recognized color system or an ink manufacturer's sample book and give *specific* ink numbers for every printing job, or you are opening yourself to some potentially costly disappointments.

11. Check swatch books before using colored ink on colored paper

Some paper manufacturers publish color-on-color swatch books. They show a number of standard colors printed on each of their colored papers in a range of values—solid color, screens of 75 percent, 50 percent, 25 percent, etc. You can't possibly know what a specific color or screen tint variation will look like printed on a particular colored stock unless you *see* it. These books answer your questions, and leave no doubt the final printed color will be exactly what you desire.

12. Be wary of certain color combinations

Using color on color can be tricky. Here are some traps for the unwary:

● Transparent rather than opaque inks can be dangerous because the underlying paper color can distort the ink color.

- When blue ink is printed on dark green paper, the type virtually can't be seen.

- Light yellow ink printed on white paper may be totally unreadable because the contrast is so limited the words can't be seen.

- Black ink on dark red may well be unreadable, too.

When in doubt, talk to your printer.

13. Don't use coated paper unless you have to

Even though many people think coated paper is endowed with some kind of supreme quality, it essentially has no character. What's worse, coated paper has one serious handicap: It reflects light and creates glare, impeding readability. It is a handicap you—and your readers—don't need.

If you *must* use a coated sheet, specify one with a dull coat and give your readers a break.

14. Know the differences between "whites"

The word *white* applied to paper is almost meaningless. Examine the "white" papers included in a number of swatch books and see for yourself the many shades of white you find.

A natural white sheet (one that isn't too bright) is friendly both to the eyes and to type, encouraging reading. A fluorescent white sheet can be blinding. Such a bright sheet could be an asset used for a poster with big, black type and rugged, dramatic illustrations. The same sheet used in a brochure with more than a minor bit of text would pose a difficult visual problem.

15. Colored paper works best with heavier faces

When type is to be printed on a colored sheet—perhaps in a colored ink—the choice of face and its size and weight can become very important. Colored papers work best with heavier faces whose elements are a uniform weight, say Bookman, rather than with a lighter face, such as Garamond.

16. Make sure the mechanicals are returned

Some printers love to keep mechanicals in their own files. To prevent this make sure printers understand they *must* return all mechanicals, undamaged, as soon as the job is completed. If you don't get your mechanicals, don't pay the bill until you do.

17. Use white prints to replace lost mechanicals

If you somehow lose your mechanicals, don't despair. Ask your printer for a set of white prints. The shop makes these by using the negatives from which the original printing plates were made. Because the print material is a white plastic that neither shrinks nor stretches, you receive a set of black and white prints fully the equal of your original mechanicals. The shop will charge for the white prints, but the cost is inconsequential compared to the expense of re-creating an entire set of mechanicals.

CHAPTER 6

Saving Money

FOR MOST OF US, using type right—so that it's easily read, so that its message comes across correctly, so that it's attractive and tasteful—also means staying within a budget. When that budget's tight, the designer and client must work together to save every penny possible.

This chapter will give you some tips for saving money that you might not have thought of—alternatives that can be used effectively without harming the design.

In addition to taking these steps, you can keep costs down by being sure your copy is prepared properly and by working with suppliers. Ask, continually, how you can prepare your work to make their job easier. Ask printers for their advice on how you can save money by preparing mechanicals or illustrations differently, for tips on reducing paper costs. Cherish those tradespeople who know their work thoroughly, use them to strengthen your grasp of the technical aspects of graphic arts—all to improve your working knowledge and thus to produce your print projects at the least cost.

1. "Batch" copy by type size and style

Don't send copy to your type shop by dribs and drabs. Each time you do, you add handling and prep costs to the project. Wait until you have enough copy to make typesetting worthwhile, then send it.

It may also pay you to separate all text copy by type size and face, and to separate all heads and display copy by size and face. By separate, I mean all 24-point heads of Garamond on one sheet of paper, all 36-point heads of Garamond on another sheet, all 36-point Helvetica heads on yet another sheet.

Sure, it means more work in your office, but it may be a lot cheaper than having the type shop do the work. Because type jobs and typesetting methods vary so greatly, you should check with your typographer to find out if, and how, batching could save you money. You may want to handle a book one way, a letterhead another, and fifty lines of heads yet another, so ask.

2. Invest in rubber stamps

For work you send through regularly, such as the text for a newsletter or magazine, you can eliminate mistakes and speed up typemarking by using a small rubber stamp that gives the basic typesetting directions, such as: 10/12 Century Expanded × 24.

Stamps save time in copy preparation and insure that the type shop will know exactly what you want.

3. Select text faces with companion italics

When you see a brochure, flip chart, or sales letter with underlining instead of italics, you know the type choice was probably faulty. With the hundreds of text faces available with companion italics, the cost of underlining—usually done by hand during paste-up—is totally unnecessary, as well as ugly and unprofessional.

Shoptalk: Establishing credibility
. . .says The Wall Street Journal

Underlining is usually unsightly and visually annoying because of, in part, the type descenders—and often is more expensive than simply using italics.

The persuasive principle
Enhancing your credibility

A special from June 15 through July 15.

4. Use stand-up, not set-in, initial letters

Set-in initials (where the top of the initial letter aligns with the ascenders in the first line of text) are always in style, but they cost extra because they take longer to set. You can avoid most of the extra cost by using stand-up initials, where the baseline aligns with the base of the first line of text. This requires that only the first line of text be altered to accommodate the initial cap. Such type treatment maximizes both appearance and ease of handling.

Fantastic, creative designs are possible using stand-up initials, and they cost less to set than set-in initials because only the first line of text has to be set to a special length.

"MERICANS have for centuries felt spiritual kinship with India," begins Stuart Cary Welch of the Fogg Art Museum in his introduction to "A Second Paradise: Indian Courtly Life 1590-1947," to be published by Doubleday this week.

5. Use white space to separate elements

Designs that call for column rules (thin lines between columns of type), "breakers" between stories, and dingbats—any element that has to be typeset or added during paste-up—can increase your costs. Don't be afraid to use white space instead. It's very apt to be cost-cutting as well as more attractive.

Where rules *must* be used, they should be typeset if possible to reduce hand setting and board costs and improve quality.

The governor rejected the state attorney general's report, saying that the advisory committee did not have access to all the facts and "was biased in a certain direction." He refused to quote specific instances where the report was faulty, but said he would appoint his own committee to look into the problem.

A spokesperson for the attorney general's office called the report "accurate and balanced" and said the formation of a new committee will only delay much-needed reforms. "The governor is responding to political pressures," the aide said. "He's the one who is biased, not this report."

The attorney general could not be reached for comment.

Leaders in both houses of the state legislature urged the governor and attorney general to resolve their differences on this issue.

Democratic leaders maintain that the governor is trying to create an issue that Republican candidates can use to their advantage in the fall election, but Republican officials deny that there is any political motive behind the delay.

"This is a serious matter that cannot be decided lightly," one high-ranking Republican said. "I don't think anyone should be criticized for trying to make sure that all the pertinent information has been gathered, and that it has been gathered by an impartial body."

The governor rejected the state attorney general's report, saying that the advisory committee did not have access to all the facts and "was biased in a certain direction." He refused to quote specific instances where the report was faulty, but said he would appoint his own committee to look into the problem.

A spokesperson for the attorney general's office called the report "accurate and balanced" and said the formation of a new committee will only delay much-needed reforms. "The governor is responding to political pressures," the aide said. "He's the one who is biased, not this report."

The attorney general could not be reached for comment.

Leaders in both houses of the state legislature urged the governor and attorney general to resolve their differences on this issue.

Democratic leaders maintain that the governor is trying to create an issue that Republican candidates can use to their advantage in the fall election, but Republican officials deny that there is any political motive behind the delay.

"This is a serious matter that cannot be decided lightly," one high-ranking Republican said. "I don't think anyone should be criticized for trying to make sure that all the pertinent information has been gathered, and that it has been gathered by an impartial body."

To save money, use white space rather than more costly rules or graphic elements to separate items. Simple alleys between columns of type can be as effective as column rules, especially if the type is justified.

6. Eliminate extra-cost boxes

If you use traditional four-sided boxes, you can increase typesetting costs. For one thing, the type must be set to a shorter measure to maintain the proper margins between the type and the rules that make the box, and that can require extra typesetting time. For another, rules must often be added by hand, usually during paste-up.

Save money by using an open box. Set type to standard column width, along with other text, and create the box by simply having column-width rules at top and bottom. You get the same effect as a full box, only far neater.

Another technique is to either overprint or doubleprint the type on a screen of box size.

(If you must have a traditional box, watch those inside margins—they *must* be equal and ample.)

A screened box like this one draws attention, but requires that the type be set narrower than the standard column width.

Attention: Advertisers
Because of the holiday, advertising deadlines for the next two issues have been changed. Display advertising for the January issue must be submitted by Dec. 1 and classified advertising by Dec. 15. Display advertising for the February issue must be submitted by Jan. 9 and classified advertising by Jan. 23. Call your advertising representative if you have any questions.

Full boxes are more expensive than open boxes. This quote in an open box is very effective.

QUOTE OF THE DAY

"How glorious it is—and also how painful—to be an exception."
—Alfred de Musset

7. Pay only for editorial changes

When proofreading galleys of type, be sure to mark all typographic errors created by the typesetters with the abbreviation *PE* for printer's error. Those the type shop pays for. Indicate editorial corrections with *AA* for author's alteration. Those you must pay for. If you don't designate printer's errors as separate from editorial changes, you could end up paying for them, too.

(If you supply copy to the type house on computer disk, all text errors will be charged to you.)

Remember: It's far cheaper to make editorial changes in manuscript before typesetting. This is the greatest area of unnecessary cost and can be the hardest to control.

8. Leave widows but fix orphans

A widow is created when the last line of a paragraph is very short, perhaps a single word or syllable. While some typographers advocate correcting all widows, this is a time-consuming, costly chore—usually not feasible. Leave all but the most odious of them.

An orphan is created when a short line falls at the top of a page or column. (The terms *widow* and *orphan* are sometimes used interchangeably.) These should be eliminated by rejuggling the page or the column lengths. A less desirable cure is to letterspace the line to create a full-length line. It isn't the best typography, but it's certainly better than leaving an orphan to fend for itself.

Widows and orphans are the bane of the paste-up person, and good typographic practice frowns on both. But it's often too costly or too time-consuming to correct them all. So leave widows like the one at the end of the first full paragraph, but correct orphans like those at the tops of these two columns—they're much more annoying.

tive read."

Watts, a subsidiary of Grolier, Inc., publishes 200 titles each year, about 40 of them coming from Breslin's division. Few manuscripts are purchased from first-time authors, but Breslin is more likely to be interested in nonfiction than fiction. "Never cut corners on your research," Breslin says. "And never send an editor—or an agent—the first or second draft of your manuscript." Breslin will consider queries for books on business and economics, history, politics and sports; don't send humor, coffee table books, cookbooks or gardening books. "The books in the catalog are a good indicator of what we'll be buying in the foreseeable future."

Terms: Pays 10, 12½ or 15% on list price. Advance "depends on the book. This past year we have paid $2,000 to more than $75,000." *Submissions:* Que-

Charles L. Wyrick Jr.

Nonfiction has the best chance of winning acceptance here, especially if it's in the areas of art, history, humor, biography or regional. "We do not normally publish works with religious topics or themes, how-to books, cookbooks, student writings or scholarly dissertations." Fiction that will be considered includes adventure, humor, experimental, mainstream or mystery, but no sci-fi, western or romance. Recent titles published include *Charleston Charlie,* a children's book, and a travel guide on Charleston.

Terms: Pays 8-15% royalty on retail price. Average royalty $250. *Submissions:* Submit either outline/synopsis and sample chapters or complete manuscript. Reports in two weeks on queries, four weeks on manuscripts. *1A Pinckney St., Box 89, Charleston, South Carolina 29402, tel. 803/722-0881.*

9. Try these color combinations

If you need the extra impact of two colors, but don't want to pay for two colors of ink, think about dark blue on light-blue textured stock or dark green on light green stock. And it's very hard to beat a dark red ink on a lively gray stock—one with some positive character, perhaps containing a touch of red to liven it up.

And here's a great way to get the effect of color on color without paying for colored stock: Select a sheet of paper with a cream tint, then print your job in brown ink, one with a bit of red in it. Dark brown on cream is an old combination, ideal for many projects.

PART THREE

LEARNING MORE

THE RULES AND GUIDELINES in this book cover the basics of good typography, but they are just the beginning. As you continue to work with type, you will add to these principles and expand your knowledge of the field. That's as it should be. Typography is an ever-changing field, one that will continue to challenge you as you conquer its subtleties and intricacies. All of us involved in working with type must continue to read and learn and grow.

This section of the book is designed to help you as you continue the learning process. Chapter 7 gives you some hints about resources and activities that offer valuable lessons for every designer. For the most part, they are ways you can expand your knowledge on your own, by surrounding yourself with good reference materials and tools, by learning from those you come into contact with as you work.

Another important tool for continuing to learn is the Glossary. Use it not only as a reference, but pursue the information within it actively. Read the definitions of terms relevant to your work and make sure you use them correctly. Then start expanding your vocabulary and, along with it, your knowledge of the field.

CHAPTER 7

Ways to Improve Your Type IQ

THE FOLLOWING PAGES contain some hints on ways to improve your typographic IQ, working essentially on your own. I think you'll find them valuable and worthwhile.

There are two important personal attributes, however, all practitioners of graphic design have to acquire on their own. You may very well have them already. I refer to good judgment and good taste. Neither comes within the covers of a single book, nor may they be purchased at an art supply shop.

Both may, however, be cultivated by reading well and widely; by reading texts such as this, then weighing what has been said, testing the author's suggestions against realistic (common sense, again!) yardsticks.

Taste is defined in my desk dictionary as, "The faculty of discerning what is aesthetically excellent or appropriate." Good judgment, on the other hand, is the faculty that enables a designer to discriminate between something aesthetically attractive and what's practical. What good is a beautiful design that no one can read?

It is the proper balancing of these two judgments that mark the graphic designer who has matured wisely and well, who is the commander of this fascinating craft.

1. Rely on good reference books

Within arm's reach at all times should be one or more style manuals that answer every tricky question of good usage. My favorite is *Words Into Type* (Prentice-Hall) for concise answers, excellent examples, and both a comprehensive table of contents and a great index. It will spare you more grief, save you more time, settle more arguments faster than you can now believe.

Also get the U.S. Government Printing Office manual, available from that office, Washington, DC, 20402. Two viewpoints may be better than one. Another highly esteemed reference is the University of Chicago's *The Chicago Manual of Style.*

No beginner in graphic arts should live without the *Pocket Pal,* a book that has been helping neophytes since 1934 when the International Paper Company first introduced it. Constantly updated, the *Pocket Pal* describes every printing process, defines technical terms, shows examples of everything from the classification of typefaces to a type family, to letterspacing and line spacing. It's the world's greatest value between paper covers.

Obtain copies of type specimen books issued by your local commercial type shops. If you buy, select, specify, or fit type, you must know what faces are available. Each manual will vary, since each shop carries a different selection of text and display faces, but all will show certain basic faces, such as Helvetica and Times Roman.

Almost without exception type manuals show complete alphabets, both capitals and lowercase, provide character counts per pica, and often show paragraphs of text in the most popular faces so that you can judge character fit, weight (color), line spacing requirements, need for minusing, and other type basics.

You can't function without these books for they are your source for locating the perfect typeface for the problem at hand. As your typographic knowledge grows, so will your library of type manuals . . . and you'll come to cherish them.

As time and your purse permit, you will acquire other references. A valuable one will illustrate in different colors and values the difference between a drop-out, reverse, overprint, and double print. These may seem overly technical, but it's to your advantage to learn the differences between them.

Paper manufacturers supply swatch books containing samples of each of their products. These books enable you to see and feel each sheet, check for opacity, select and specify the exact weight and grade of paper you wish. Your printer and paper distributor sales reps (ask them about a mill visit) will help you learn how to use them.

2. Develop a crib file

Perhaps it's a treatment of an initial letter that catches your eye. You've never seen it done before, but it's a delight. Clip and file.

Perhaps you spot a color combination of inks and text paper that impresses you. Drop it in the file.

Maybe you find a typeface used in an advertisement for a product similar to one your client manufactures. The face has the charisma, the character you are trying to get across. Clip it out.

Your crib file should include examples of good typography that catch your eye—any item you can show a client and say, "This is the kind of design I feel this new project needs. It will make the impact on readers we need to make."

I'm not advocating stealing designs or using other people's art for your own project. Paper, an ink color, a combination of ink and paper, type tricks, new typefaces, a smashing mix of unusual typefaces . . . all can be grist for your mill. All can be used years (or hours) later, perhaps to show exactly what it is you want when you can't put it into words.

There's no substitute for a good crib file . . . to stimulate, inspire, instruct!

Whenever you see an interesting bit of typography, clip it and put it in a file. Then turn to that file any time you need guidance or inspiration.

3. Go to school

Many schools now run night and weekend classes, seminars and workshops, and you may well discover basic courses you can take, such as: introduction to graphic design, copyfitting, designing with type, fundamentals of paper, and proofreading. Rochester Institute of Technology has offered a three-day seminar with the intriguing title, "Printing for people who aren't printers and probably never will be."

4. Plan a study program

If the classes you want aren't readily available, don't give up. You can learn a great deal by visiting suppliers. Spend a day at a local print shop, perhaps a shop you work with. Promise not to get into the workers' hair, but to observe and to question only when it won't interfere. You'll return to your office full of new and valuable knowledge.

Repeat the procedure with any other supplier who'll let you in: the shop that does color separations, the firm producing 35mm slides, the video studio doing a show for a client's next sales meeting. Try the trade bindery that does special work most printers no longer perform, the type shop that does your typesetting. Many shops work one or more night shifts, so you can often visit on your own time. When you're learning, don't ignore any aspect of the process. For example: You may never do mark-up to prepare copy for typesetting, but having a mark-up specialist explain what he or she is doing and why will open your eyes.

5. Set type by hand, run a job press or a paper cutter

By far the best way to learn about type and typesetting and to appreciate it, is to set type by hand. Find a hobbyist with his or her own shop and ask to be taken on as an unpaid apprentice. It's an unforgettable experience to belly up to a California Job Case (a case designed to hold metal type), learn the case layout as you work, and absorb the basics.

The same hobbyist may well have a hand-fed job press and you can learn the rudiments of make-ready, imposition, gauge setting, inking, and other delights of producing your first printed item. Some small shops also have hand-operated paper cutters, providing you the chance to learn still another special skill.

6. Learn the vocabulary

If someone yells across the office to a designer, "Make it bleed top and bottom," don't expect to see blood flow. It's simply a direction to have the illustration, rule, or whatever run off the page at the top and bottom.

The thirteenth edition of *Pocket Pal* carries twenty-seven pages of general graphic arts terms, not all of which will concern you. Pick out the ones you should know and memorize them. The same advice applies to the glossary beginning on page 96. The knowledge you gain will save you time and money and prevent errors, for the exact technical term always beats the ambiguous.

7. Buy a pica ruler

Invest in an 18-inch stainless steel ruler known as a pica ruler or line gauge. It has inches and picas on opposite edges of the face. A good one will probably have 8-point and agate type markings on the back edges, plus slots within the body of the ruler showing various type sizes, as well as tenths of an inch. Look on the purchase as a lifetime investment.

Also useful is a slightly less expensive but excellent 18-inch plastic graphic arts ruler that shows screen values as percentages of 110-line screen and half-tone screens from 55- to 150-line. One brand shows proofreaders' marks, picas to inches conversion, and throws in a handy pica vs. 10- and 12-pitch typewriter character count, plus more.

As long as you are talking type, or specifying type, stick to picas and points and you will have no problems. When you deal with engravers and paper merchants, however, remember that they deal in inches, never having adopted the point system.

8. Become conscious of graphic designs

Learn to *look* at advertisements, art, graphic elements such as bar charts, initial letters, line drawings, pencil sketches, color prints. Study them, see what makes them work. Use your common sense in judging them and try to figure out what (if anything) went wrong.

If the full-color picture of a New Hampshire scene shows birches with yellow or green bark, then it's bad printing (usually) or improper color separations.

If you lose your place when your eye attempts to drop to the next line of text, it may well be the line was set too wide for its type size or, often, there isn't enough white space between the lines.

If you are confronted with columns of type in a magazine with no subheads to provide relief or add editorial clarity, you're faced with an unimaginative editor or, at the least, an untutored one.

If you respond warmly to a well-designed book or advertisement, study them; consider what made you respond positively. It will be knowledge well gained and perhaps items to add to your clip file.

9. Read, and look ahead

Today, and every day, we are in the midst of change: in ways to print, to set type, to transmit information . . . the latest technical revolutions are now underway. You *must* always be aware of those changes that will affect you and your career. Don't wait for someone in authority to ask if you have explored, have considered, some new typesetting or printing technique.

The smartest answer is not, "I'm planning to look into it." You must be able to say, "Yes, I have been watching the development carefully," and toss in some specifics if appropriate. The career you save may be your own.

Consider each new idea as part of your printing "education." And remember, Robert Frost once said, "Education is what you have left after you've forgotten all you've learned."

Typography Glossary

AA. Author's alteration. Used in proofing to indicate any change in original copy that is not a typesetter's error.

Accent. Mark used to indicate pronunciation in phonetic guide or languages other than English.

Agate. Now used mostly as a measurement for newspaper advertising. Originally the name for 5½-point type, 14 agate lines equal one inch.

Align or alignment. To line up type horizontally (usually along the bottom or the baseline). Also alignment of any graphic element with another.

Alley. Space between two columns of typeset material.

Alphabet length. Length measurement of the lowercase alphabet, usually used to compare character counts of different typefaces.

Alphanumeric. Combining letters and numbers. Contraction of *alphabet* and *numeric.*

Alternate character. Nonstandard character available with some typefaces. Swash capitals and lowercase letters with shorter or longer ascenders and descenders are examples.

Monotype's Caslon Old Style Italic shows the alternate characters available—in this case, swash letters.

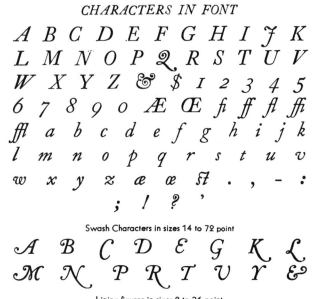

CHARACTERS IN FONT

A B C D E F G H I J K
L M N O P Q R S T U V
W X Y Z & $ 1 2 3 4 5
6 7 8 9 0 Æ Œ fi ff fl ffi
ffl a b c d e f g h i j k
l m n o p q r s t u v
w x y z æ œ st . , - :
; ! ? '

Swash Characters in sizes 14 to 72 point

A B C D E G K L
M N P R T U Y &

Lining figures in sizes 8 to 36 point
42 to 72 point fonts contain lining figures only.

Courtesy of Composing Room of New England.

Ampersand. Symbol (&) also called "short and" and used as substitute for the word *and.*

Antique finish. A rough, natural surface on paper.

Arabic number. Numerals 0 – 9. Compare Roman numeral.

Artwork. Those elements of a printed item that are illustrative or decorative, as distinguished from text.

Ascending letter. Type character having letter strokes rising above x-height, such as *t, l, b, d.*

Author's alteration. See AA.

Author's proof. Clean proof for author after typographic errors have been corrected.

Back matter. Materials following main text of a book, such as index and appendix.

Bad break. Applied, usually, to incorrect word division, but also when column starts with last line of preceding paragraph.

Banner. Headline running across entire page; a screamer. Sometimes used incorrectly to refer to a newspaper's title. Compare Flag, Masthead, Nameplate.

Baseline. Imaginary horizontal line (bottom of x-height) which all type characters in a line must touch.

Bastard title. Book title, standing alone, and appearing before full title page. Also called half title.

b/b or b to b. Abbreviation for baseline to baseline. Used to indicate line spacing.

bf. Proofer's mark indicating boldface.

Binding. The process of fastening pages together to create a book, pamphlet, or booklet. To bind with wire, adhesive, thread, or other means.

Black-letter. Applied to early typefaces designed to look like early German handwriting. Often referred to as Old English.

Bleed. Printed area such as a photograph or tint allowed to run off the edge of the trimmed sheet.

Blind embossing. Stamped design incorporating no color; a bas-relief. See Embossing.

Block quote. See Extract.

Blowup. Photographic enlargement.

Blue. Pre-press proof printed in blue; submitted by offset printer and made by exposing negatives against sensitized paper. Also called vandykes when printed in brown. See Saltprint.

Bodoni dash. Also called a tapered dash. Thicker in the center and thinner on ends.

Body type. Typeset text or copy, usually ranging from 6- to 14-point type, used as reading matter and set in one face. Compare Display type.

Boldface. Heavier-weight version of a typeface; indicated by proofreader's mark (bf).

Bond paper. High-quality paper usually used for letterhead and business forms and having strength and durability.

Border. Plain or ornamental frame around any typographic element.

Boxed. Frame around type element, either "open" with rules top and bottom only, or on all four sides.

Box head. Column heading enclosed in rules.

Brace or bracket. Characters used in pairs to embrace type and available in many sizes, both plain and ornamental. Braces: { }   Brackets: [ ]

Brady's Golden Rule. "Space together those things that go together." All elements that relate to each other must be shown to do so visually.

Break. Place where division is made, such as ending of line, division of type column.

Breakout. Material pulled from text and displayed as quotation in larger or bolder type for emphasis. Also called pull-quote.

Brightness. The brilliance of a sheet of printing paper; its light-reflecting quality.

Broadside. Large sheet of paper, commonly printed on one side, sometimes folded. Often used for advertising circulars.

Bulking. Degree of paper thickness.

Bullet. Type character, usually round, used to draw attention, particularly in lists.

California Job Case. Case for handset type, holding both upper and lower-case characters, plus figures, spaces, and related characters.

Calligraphic type. Typefaces based on styles of handwriting, such as Slogan, Legend, Brush.

Callout. Label used on illustration, sometimes with a line pointing to specific portion of illustration.

Camera ready. Material ready to be photographed. See Mechanical.

Cap height. Actual height of capital letter, as opposed to its point size. Sometimes used in type specifications. See Type size.

Capital. Large letters of the alphabet, also termed caps, uppercase and, anciently, majuscules.

Caps and small caps. Two sizes of matching capitals made in one size of type, available with many fonts. Small caps are the same height as the lower case "x." Abbreviated as c/sc.

Caption. A title and/or a short explanation or description adjacent to an illustration or photograph. See Legend and Cutlines.

Caret. Mark (∧) used by copyeditors and proofreaders to indicate where material is to be inserted.

Casting off. Estimating the space typewritten copy will occupy when set in a specific size typeface.

Chapter head. Display heading appearing at the beginning of a chapter.

Character. A letter of the alphabet, number, punctuation mark, etc. Also, the quality inherent in design of each typeface and projected to reader.

Character count. Average number of type characters in a line, page, manuscript, publication, etc.

Characters-per-pica. Average number of characters that will fit in one pica for individual typefaces; used to calculate the length copy will be when set in a given typeface.

Circular. A printed advertisement—booklet, leaflet, or letter—distributed to a large number of persons.

Clip art. Illustrative material which can be purchased and used by "clipping" from supplied camera-ready material. Also termed stock art. Some types available on floppy diskette.

Close spacing. Thin spacing between words.

Close up. To reduce space between graphic elements, such as type lines.

Coated paper. Papers with surface coatings that produce ultrasmooth finishes, ranging from matte to super-glossy.

Cold type. Composition achieved by direct impression, such as a typewriter or a word processor-printer combination. Sometimes called "strike-on" composition. See Hot type.

Color. See Weight.

Color separation. Separation of color original into the four primary printing color components: yellow, red (magenta), blue (cyan), black.

Column rule. Line used to separate columns of type.

Composition. Typesetting.

Comprehensive layout. A "comp"—carefully prepared layout or dummy finished to closely approximate the look of the planned printed piece.

Computerized typesetting. General term for typesetting that uses computers to automatically hyphenate, justify, and do page formatting.

Condensed type. A typeface thinner than normal, often prepared as a variation of a standard face. Compare Expanded type.

Continuous tone. Any illustration or photograph containing varied tones, either shades of gray from black to white, or color. Continuous tone art must be converted to halftone screens before printing.

Contour. Type set to wrap around another element or create an unusual shape. Also called run-around.

Copy. Text, usually typewritten or computer produced, from which type is to be composed. Also, general term for text.

Copyfitting. Determining the space a given amount of copy will fill when set in a specific typeface and size. Also, selecting or adjusting typeface and size to fit a predetermined space.

Copy preparation. Editing copy to insure all style and other typographic directions are indicated properly before typesetting.

Counter. Opening within a type character.

Cover paper, or stock. Heavier weight stock used for covers of booklets, catalogs, and similar items; often available with matching text paper.

Cromalins. Brand name for full-color proofs made before printing from special positive film.

Crop. To mark for removal, or to remove, unwanted portions of a photograph or illustration.

Cursive. A type that imitates handwriting, such as Bernhard Cursive.

Cut-in head. Heading set into text, either partly or entirely.

Cutline. Short description or explanation adjacent to an illustration or photograph, other than a title or heading. Usually used in reference to newspapers. Also see Legend and Caption.

Cut-off rule. Printed line used to separate advertisements from news items or other elements. Also called advertising rule.

Cyan. The blue primary color used in four-color process printing.

Counters are the open spaces in letters. Note the extreme difference in the counters of the capital *A* in these three examples.

Courtesy of Composing Room of New England.

Dagger. Single (†) and double (‡) reference marks.

Debossed. Depressed (recessed) design, the opposite of embossed (raised).

Deckle edge. Untrimmed feathery edges of paper, available on some grades of paper and cover stock.

Delete. Proofreader's mark meaning to eliminate designated item.

Descending letter. Letter stroke that extends below baseline, such as *p, y, j.*

Diacritic. Mark used to indicate accent or pronunciation.

Die-stamping. Printing, often letterheads and business cards, from designs engraved into copper or steel plates.

Digital (digitized) typesetting. Typesetting system where characters are translated into a collection of tiny dots or lines that can be stored in computer memory as binary codes. Image quality is determined by density of strokes or scan lines per inch as reproduced on cathode ray tube, prior to transfer to film or paper.

Dingbat. Any small printer's ornament, such as a floret.

Display type. General term for type set larger than surrounding text (usually 14-point or larger) as in headings or advertisements.

Double-truck. Two facing pages, designed as a single unit. Also called spread.

Down style. Style of headline with only the first word and proper nouns capitalized.

Down-style heads use capital letters only for the first word and any proper nouns.

Three stores cited for customer service

In July, three stores—No. 008, No. 131, and No. 162—were awarded the company's Outstanding Customer Service Award. Employees of each of the three stores were treated to a dinner banquet in recognition of the award.

Drop cap. Another term for initial cap.

Drop-out. Section of mechanicals or art, such as background areas or guide lines, often designed so they will not print.

Dropped-out type. Type reversed into a background, e.g., white letters with a black background.

Dummy. Preliminary layout prepared to show position of illustrations and text as they will appear in the final reproduction. Also, set of blank pages, perhaps of a booklet, made up to show size, shape, and specific paper stock.

Duotone. A two-color halftone made from a one-color photograph.

Dupe. A duplicate negative. Also duplicate proof, slide, or other item.

Duplex paper. Paper having different color or finish on each side.

Elite. Standard typewriter type having 12 characters per inch.

Ellipsis. Three periods (. . .) used to indicate an omission of words or a pause.

Em. A unit of measurement that is as wide and as tall as the typeface being set. In 12-point type, the em is 12 points wide and 12 points high.

Em space. A fixed amount of white space equal to one em. Also called em quad.

Embossed finish. Papers having raised surfaces, often to simulate linen, wood, or leather finish, for example.

Embossing. Special process to create raised image on the surface of the paper. See Blind embossing.

En. Unit of measurement that is one-half the width of an em.

Expanded or extended type. A typeface whose characters are wider than usual, often a wider version of a regular face.

Extract. A quotation typographically set off from main body of text. Also called block quote. Sometimes referred to as pull-quote.

Many typefaces have versions that are expanded (with wider letters) or condensed (with narrower letters).

Century Schoolbook

Typography

Century expanded

Typography

Century Bold condensed

Typography

Face. Originally the printing surface of metal type, now another term for typeface.

Family. See Type family.

Felt side. The smoother, or top, side of a sheet of paper.

Fixed spacing. Uniform word spacing throughout a block of type.

F/L. Flush left.

Flag. 1. Newspaper masthead, containing staff information. 2. Note attached to manuscript page with editor's queries to author.

Flat. The assembled film negatives or positives, ready for offset platemaking. Also, an adjective describing an item lacking in contrast, such as a photograph.

Flop. To reverse negative, giving mirror-image reversal of photograph or other item.

Floret. Flower- or leaf-shaped type ornament.

Flush left or right. Typeset lines that align vertically, either left or right, and are uneven on the other end.

Flush paragraph. Paragraph having no indentation.

Folio. Page number.

Follow copy. Instruction to set type exactly as it appears in the copy, in every detail.

Font. Complete assortment of type of one face and one size, including upper- and lowercase letters, punctuation, numerals.

Footnote. Reference or explanatory material placed at bottom of type page, usually preceded by reference mark keyed to same reference mark in text.

Foreword. Introductory statement by author or other person.

Format. The size, shape, form, proportions, margins, and overall design of a printed item.

Foundry type. Type cast in complete fonts in a foundry using more durable typemetal, as contrasted with individual, hot-type characters cast on a Monotype.

Four-color press. A press that prints four wet colors in a single pass.

F/R. Flush right.

Free-standing insert. Printed material inserted into a magazine or newspaper that is not attached.

Front matter. All material preceding the main text of a book.

Full measure. Type set to fill full line length, flush at both ends.

Galley proof. Proof of typeset material before being made up into pages.

Gothic. Style of plain typeface usually having just one weight of line. Example: News Gothic. Also, sometimes used to refer to black-letter typefaces. The term is confusing because it's used for two different type styles.

Grain. The direction in which most paper fibers lie, corresponding to the direction the fibers point when still wet on a paper machine.

Gravure. Printing process using etched plates with intaglio (sunken or depressed) printing images. Provides excellent color reproduction; expensive.

Grease pencil. A pencil with a waxlike base. Markings can be easily removed with tissue. Used to mark photographs, etc. Also called china marker.

Greeking. Nonsense text used to simulate actual text placement and size during planning stages.

Grid. Series of lines in nonreproducible blue ink printed on paste-up board indicating placement of text and illustrations. The grid dictates such considerations as column width and margins.

Gutter. Inner margins between type and binding.

Hairline. Term for very fine or delicate line, the finest printer's rule.

Hairline register. Register within one-half row of dots; in general, very close register.

Half title. See Bastard title.

Halftone. Continuous-tone art (a photograph, for example) converted into dots of various sizes for reproduction.

H & J. Hyphenate and justify. Computer function that creates type with even edges on both the left and right.

Hanging figures. See Old-style figures.

Hanging indentation. First line of paragraph set full length and all following lines indented.

Hanging punctuation. Punctuation set in margins, outside of justified line length, so that text aligns optically.

Hanging quote. Opening quote mark placed in left margin beyond justified line length.

Hard copy. Printed copy of text stored in computer memory. Often used as a permanent visual record. Also, typewritten material sent to composing house for typesetting.

Head or heading. Display line usually set in a larger size or different typeface than text, summarizing text below and used to draw attention.

Headline. Title or caption of a newspaper article, usually set in display type.

Head margin. White space above first type line appearing on page.

Holding line. See Keyline.

Hot metal or type. Type set by using molten metal to form either individual letters (Monotype) or a complete line of letters (Linotype, Ludlow). Becoming outdated as phototypesetting gains popularity.

House style. Rules governing punctuation, spelling, spacing, etc., set up by publisher to insure consistent usage.

Hung initial. Initial letter set in left-hand margin, in whole or in part.

Hyphenate and justify. See H & J.

Imposition. Positioning of pages during printing so that after printing and folding pages are in consecutive order. See Signature.

Indent. Placing space before or after words in type line (example, paragraph indent).

Index. Alphabetized listing of names, places, and subjects included in a printed work, giving the page number on which each item is mentioned.

Inferior character. Small character placed below baseline, as in a chemical formula: H_2O. Also, subscript.

Initial cap. The first text letter set larger than remaining text and either plain or decorated. Used for emphasis or design. Also called drop cap.

Inline. A type letter with a white line, such as Goudy Handtooled.

Insert. An item, usually printed, placed in a publication, either bound, tipped in, or free standing. Also, additional material added to a manuscript.

Italic. Slanted letters, as distinct from roman letters, used for emphasis and other purposes. Often abbreviated as *ital*.

Jump head. Headline over news story continued from a preceding page.

Justify. Set type so that all lines are the same length creating even edges on both the left and right. Compare Ragged left, Ragged right.

Kerning. Subtracting space between certain combinations of type characters to tighten fit and improve appearance. Done on case-by-case basis according to need. Compare Minusing.

Some combinations of letters need to be set more closely together to improve fit. This is called kerning and here are a few examples.

AC AT AV AW AY FA LT LV LW LY OA OV OW OY PA
L' L- L— P. P, P; P: P- P— R- R— Ta Te Ti To Tr Tu Tw T
Wo Wr Wu Wy W. W, W; W: W- W— Ya Ye Yi Yo Yu Y
AG AO AQ AU BA BE BL BP BR BU BV BW BY CA
EC EO FC FG FO GE GO GR GU HO IC IG IO JA JO
OH OI OK OL OM ON OP OR OT OU OX PE PL PO

Courtesy of CPC Type and Graphics, Southboro, MA.

Key. To use letters or symbols to code copy to a layout. Similar methods are used to indicate text insertions, etc.

Keyline. 1. Outline on mechanical to indicate shape and position of artwork or photographs. Also called holding lines. 2. Entire mechanical. 3. Process of pasting up elements on mechanical.

Lacquer. A clear coating (gloss or dull) applied to a printed sheet to enhance image, or for protection.

Laid paper. Paper showing a pattern of parallel lines to simulate the pattern created by screens in handmade paper. Unlined paper is referred to as wove paper.

Layout. The plan or design of a proposed printed piece showing how all elements will be arranged.

Leaders. Series of dots, dashes, or periods used to "lead" the eye across the page from one type column to another. See Open leaders.

Leader dots "lead" the eye from one item to another.

Contents

Leading (ledding). The distance between type lines, measured in points from the baseline of one line of type to the baseline of the next line. Also, Linespacing.

Leading is the amount of space between lines of type.

12-point type plus 2 points of leading
12-point type plus 2 points of leading

12-point type set solid
12-point type set solid

Leaf. As bound in a book, a single sheet of paper, each side of which is a page.

Leaflet. A single sheet, sometimes folded, but not bound.

Legend. Words under illustration, briefly describing it. Also, see Cutline, Caption.

Legibility. Related to speed with which each letter or word can be recognized.

Letterpress. Printing from raised blocks or type. Ink is spread on the raised surface and paper is pressed against it to form the image.

Letterset. A dry offset printing process using a relief plate similar to that used in letterpress and requiring no dampening system.

Letterspacing. The space between letters; can be increased or decreased to achieve special effects. Usually used to refer to the addition of space between letters.

Ligature. Two or more typeface characters connected to form a single unit, as in ff.

Line art or line drawing. Illustration, such as pen and ink drawing, suitable for reproduction without using a halftone.

Line length or measure. Length of a type line, given in picas.

Linespacing. See leading.

Lining figures. Figures that align at the bottom, unlike old-style figures, which have ascenders and descenders.

Linotype. A hot metal typesetting system that sets one line at a time.

Lithography. Printing from a flat surface, where the image area is receptive to ink and the rest of the surface is not.

A logotype, such as this neat one for Andover Bank, is used to establish a company's identity.

Andover Bank

Logotype. Also called logo. The name, symbol, or trademark of a company or publication as a single design unit.

Lowercase (lc). Small letters as distinguished from capitals; so termed because they were stored in the lower of the two wooden type cases used by hand compositors. Anciently, minuscule.

Ludlow. A hot-metal typesetting machine used mainly for hand setting lines of display type and headlines.

Magenta. In four-color process, one of the primaries; red.

Majuscule. Capital letter.

Makeready. Work done to prepare press and printing plates or forms prior to running, such as setting paper feeder, grippers, side guide, filling and adjusting ink fountains, etc.

Makeup. In letterpress, arrangement of all elements—type, space, and illustrations—into final form for reproduction.

Margin. White space on all four sides of a printed page.

Markup. Placing all appropriate instructions on copy and layout to insure proper typesetting. Also "Spec"-ing.

Masthead. Listing in newspaper, magazine, or other publication of information about staff, operation, date and volume number, address, etc. Also called flag.

Matte finish. Coated paper having dull finish, without gloss or luster.

Matte print. Photoprint with dull finish.

Measure. Length of a type line, given in picas.

Mechanical. An assemblage or pasteup on art board of all elements needed to create printed item. Photographed to create printing plate.

Minuscule. Small or lowercase letter.

Minusing. Decreasing space between type characters. Also called squeezing and tracking. Done throughout text rather than on case-by-case basis. Compare Kerning.

Minusing or squeezing type is done by cutting down the white space between letters. The top alphabet is set in Cheltenham Book normal. The second is minus one-half unit and the third is minus one unit.

abcdefghijklmnopqrstuvwxyz

abcdefghijklmnopqrstuvwxyz

abcdefghijklmnopqrstuvwxyz

Modern roman. Typefaces designed near end of 18th century, distinguished from old-style roman by greater regularity of shapes, more precise curves, vertical weight stress, and delicate hairlines and serifs. One example is Bodoni.

Bodoni is considered the first modern roman typeface.

Courtesy of Wrightson Typographers, Boston, Mass.

Montage. Photographs or other items randomly arranged to create pleasing design. Elements used can be cut to various shapes, angled, overlapped, or variously treated.

Mottled. Spotty or uneven appearance of inked surface, most easily seen in solid areas.

Ms. Abbreviation for manuscript. Plural is mss.

Mutt or mutton quad. Substitute term for em space, to avoid confusion with en space when spoken.

Nameplate. Type treatment of the newspaper or newsletter name, usually displayed at the top of page one. Also called banner.

Negative. Film containing reverse image; dark areas appear light and light, dark.

Newsprint. Paper used mostly for printing newspapers.

Nonrepro blue. A light blue color that is not picked up by the reproductive camera. Used to mark corrections on mechanicals.

Nut quad. Substitute term for en space, to avoid confusion with spoken word em.

Oblong binding. Book bound on the shorter side.

Offset. Short for offset lithography. Printing process in which inked image is first transferred (offset) from a plate cylinder to a blanket cylinder, then from the blanket to paper. See also Lithography.

Old English. A black-letter typeface based on 13th-century German writing styles.

Old-style. Type style developed in the sixteenth and seventeenth centuries. Bold strokes of uniform thickness and rounded or sloping serifs. Caslon is one example.

Old-style figures. Numerals with ascenders and descenders. Also called hanging figures. Compare Lining figures.

Numerals with ascenders and descenders, like the Hadriano figures shown here, are called old-style figures.

$1234567890

Courtesy of Composing Room of New England.

Opacity. Paper property that minimizes the "show-through" of printed image either from back side or next sheet.

Opaque ink. Ink that conceals color over which it is printed.

Open box. A box around type or other material formed by rules on top and bottom only rather than all four sides.

Open leaders. Sometimes called dot leaders because widely spaced periods are placed in a line to lead the eye across the page.

Open spacing. Wide spacing, as between lines of display type.

Ornament. A small type decoration such as a floret or dingbat.

Orphan. See Widow.

Overlay. Clear plastic covering over mechanical holding additional material, usually in register.

Overprinting. Printing over an area already printed.

Overset. Type set but not used.

Page proof. Proof of completed type page.

Pagination. Numbering of pages in consecutive order. In computerized typesetting, automatic page make-up.

Pamphlet. An unbound printed folder or brochure.

Paragraph mark. An editing mark (¶) used to indicate the beginning of a new paragraph. Really the cap letter P, reversed. Paragraphs sometimes are indicated like this: ⌐New paragraph begins here.

Paste-up. Process of arranging type and illustrations on art board in preparation for printing. Also used to refer to mechanicals.

PE. Printer's error. Used by proofreaders to designate a mistake made in typesetting.

Perfect binding. A method of binding, without stitching or sewing, in which the pages are held together by a flexible adhesive.

Photogravure. See Gravure.

Photostat. Brand name for photocopying process. Also used generically to refer to any economically reproduced photographs or line art, often enlarged or reduced, and often used for layouts and dummies, cropped, to show size and position. Commonly referred to as stats.

Phototypesetting or photocomposition. A method of setting type photographically.

Pica. 1. A unit of measure used in typesetting. Approximately ⅙th of an inch. Compare Point. 2. Typewriter type providing ten characters per inch.

Pi character. Special typeface character such as accent mark not usually included in a standard type font, but available when required to be inserted by compositor.

Point. Unit of type measurement. One point is approximately equal to $\frac{1}{72}$nd of an inch. Twelve points equal one pica.

Point size. See Type size.

Positive. Film with light and dark values the same as original. See Negative.

Pre-press proof. Proof, such as saltprint, created by a variety of prepress means, thus saving money and time.

Press proof. Proof made on press prior to production run.

Press type. Alphabets on a clear plastic sheet in a wide range of typefaces, plus rules, borders and ornaments, etc., which can be transferred by rubbing. Also called transfer or rub-down type.

Process colors. Inks used in process printing to create the full range of colors. In four-color printing they are yellow, magenta (red), cyan (blue), and black.

Process printing. Printing where two or more colors of ink are used to create intermediate colors. Filters are used to separate color illustrations into the primary colors, then during printing one color of transparent ink is printed on top of another to re-create the effect of full color. See Process colors.

Progressive proof. Commonly termed "prog." Proof of color process work showing each color in sequence. Example: Proof of yellow plate, proof of magenta plate, then proof of yellow overprinted with magenta, etc.

Proof. Trial sheet of printed material (prepared a number of ways) for comparison against original and on which corrections are made.

Proofreader. Person who checks typeset galleys against manuscript for mistakes.

Proofreader's mark. Graphic instruction made by proofreader to indicate typesetter's errors.

Proportional spacing. Each letter has its own width, i.e., larger for letters such as *M* or *w*; smaller for characters such as *I* or *1*.

Pull-quote. Words "pulled" from text and displayed as quotation.

Quad. Space in typeset copy. Originally, metal pieces used to create space in hot type. Can also be used as a direction: quad (space) right, quad (space) left, etc.

Rag content. Indication of good paper quality. Twenty-five percent is common for business stationery.

Ragged center. Type set with each line centered.

Ragged left. Type set with the right margin even and the left margin uneven.

Ragged right. Type set with the left margin even and the right margin uneven.

Raised initial. Initial letter projecting above first line of text type. Also called stick-up or stand-up initial.

Readability. Relative ease with which a printed page can be read.

Recto. Right-hand, odd-numbered pages in book. Page one is always a right-hand page. Opposite to verso.

Reference mark. Mark used to indicate footnotes, such as asterisk or dagger.

Register. Placing one image in exact alignment with another during printing. Often done so that the two images form one when printed.

Register marks. Crosses or other marks placed on mechanicals, art, overlays, and plates to insure proper positioning.

Relief printing. Another term for letterpress. So called because printing surface is raised above non-printing areas, forming a relief.

Reproduction proof. A type proof that is camera ready. Also referred to as repro or repro proof.

Reversal illustration. Achieved by flopping negative so image will face left rather than right, or vice versa.

Reversed type. See Dropped-out type.

Revised proof. Proof taken after corrections are made. Also called second proof.

River. An irregular pattern of white space running through several successive lines of text. Considered undesirable.

RL. Ragged left.

Roman numeral. Numeral from an ancient Roman counting system based on the characters I, V, X, L, C, D, and M.

Roman type. 1. Type that is upright, as opposed to italic. 2. Type based on ancient Roman lettering. Features upright letters, variable width elements, and letter strokes ending in serifs.

Rotogravure. See Gravure.

Rough. Preliminary layout or sketch meant to give general effect.

RR. Ragged right.

Rubber cement. Used to affix material to mechanicals. See Wax and Spray Mount.

Rule. Line used for borders, boxes, and many other purposes, varying in design and thickness, usually specified in points.

Rule box. Type or other material enclosed on all four sides by a rule. See Open box.

Run-around. Type lines set to fit around illustration or other element of the design. Also called contour or wrap-around.

Run-in head. Heading set into first text line, usually set in larger size, bold, italic, or otherwise displayed.

Running head. A headline or title repeated on each page, usually at the top, sometimes includes folio.

Saddle stitch (wire). To bind a booklet or pamphlet by inserting wire stitches through the middle fold of the sheets.

Saltprints. Common term for all prepress proofs made by exposing negatives against sensitized paper. See Vandyke, Blue.

Sans serif. Letterforms without serifs and usually having a single thickness of line.

Scaling. Determining the proper size of an image to be reduced or enlarged to fit given area.

Scanner. Electronic device used to produce color and tone-corrected color separations.

Screen. A pattern of dots or lines used to reproduce continuous tone illustrations such as photographs or to create an illusion of tone. Screens are measured in numbers of lines per inch; in general, the larger number of lines per inch, the better the reproduction quality.

Screened print. A print containing a halftone screen. See Velox.

Script. Typefaces based on handwritten letters. Example: Commercial Script.

One example of a script face. Note the extreme delicacy of the thin elements.

One If By Land

Second proof, or galley. Proof taken after corrections are made.

Serif. Ending strokes of characters; short cross lines at the ends of main strokes.

Set-in initial. Large initial letter indented into text. Also termed cut-in initial.

Set-off. Ink from one printed sheet rubbing off, marking the next sheet. Also called offsetting.

Shadowmark. Economical substitute for watermark. Applied to paper after manufacture; can be in fixed position on stationery.

Show-through. Printing on the reverse side of sheet that can be seen through the sheet under normal viewing conditions.

Side head. A heading set to one side of the type page or column. A heading cut into the outer margin of text, wholly or partially, is termed a cut-in side heading.

Side wire (stitch). To wire or stitch the sheets or signatures of a book or pamphlet on the side, close to the backbone. Compare Saddle stitch.

Signature. A sheet on which several pages have been printed. After it has been folded, contents appear in correct sequence. Signatures commonly contain 12, 16, 32, or 64 pages.

Silhouette. An illustration with all background removed.

Sink. The first line of text is lower on the page than standard, as on chapter openings.

Slash mark. A diagonal mark (/) used to separate alternatives, as in and/or; to represent the word *per*, as in miles/hour; and to indicate the ends of verse lines printed continuously. Also called virgule.

Slug. A strip of metal used for spacing letterpress material, usually 6-, 12-, 18-, or 24-points in thickness. Also, a heading used to identify an article or department in a magazine.

Small caps. Smaller capital letters provided with many fonts. The size of the x-height, they usually are used in combination with the regular capitals.

Solid. 1. Large inked area. 2. Type set without extra leading.

Space out. Inserting space between words or letters to make line fill predetermined length.

Spec. Short for type specifications. Plural form sometimes written as spex. Also used as verb meaning to mark copy for typesetting, indicating size, typeface, etc.

Spine. The part of the binding that connects the two covers. Also called backbone.

Spiral binding. Method of binding in which a continuous piece of wire or plastic in spiral form is inserted through holes punched along the binding edge.

Spray Mount. Brand of spray adhesive commonly used in preparing mechanicals. Often used generically to indicate any brand of spray adhesive.

Squeeze. Set text with less than normal spacing between characters. Also see Minusing, Tracking.

Stand-up initial. Initial letter inserted only in first line of text. Also stick-up capital.

When a stand-up or stick-up initial is used, only the first line of text is indented.

Hardly a day goes by that you don't feel it. You sense it first as a gnawing, a faint uneasiness. Then you feel queasy—and maybe light in the head. Your eyes blur and you can't concentrate. Consumed by a strange numbness, you fear you may be on the verge of a stroke or a heart attack.

Stapling. Insertion of wire staples for binding. See Side wire and Saddle stitch.

Stat. See Photostat.

Stem. The main upright stroke of a letter.

Stet. Term used by copyeditors and proofreaders meaning "Let the original stand."

Stock. Paper or other material to receive printed image.

Stock art. Another term for clip art.

Strike-on composition. Prepared by direct impression, such as a typewriter.

Stripping. Positioning negatives or positives in preparation for making offset printing plate.

Subhead. Secondary headline or title.

Subscript. Undersized characters ($_3$) placed below baseline, usually for reference purposes. Also called Inferior characters.

Sunken initial. An initial letter indented into text so that its top aligns with top of ascending letters of first type line.

Superior character. Undersized character (^{3}) placed at top of type line, often for footnote reference. Also called superscript.

Swash letter. Italic capital letter with flourishes furnished with some fonts as alternate characters.

Swatch book. Book containing sample sheets of paper stock showing choices of weights, sizes, and finishes.

Tabloid. Small size newspaper, about half the size of standard newspaper. Sometimes called tab.

Text. The main body matter of a page or book, usually under 14-point, as distinguished from headings, titles, etc.

Text paper. Used for much commercial printing; usually supplied in $25'' \times 38''$ size, featuring a wide variety of colors and surfaces.

Thin space. Any space thinner than a 3-to-the-em space. Usually ¼ or ⅕ of an em space.

Thumbnail sketches. Small sketches made by graphic artist to show varied approaches to a layout or design.

Tint. A light shade of color, usually achieved by screening.

Tip-in. An illustration or other item pasted by hand, often at upper edge only, onto a book page.

Tissue layout. Rough layout on tissue prepared before typesetting to show how design project will be handled. Often done as preliminary step to preparing comprehensive.

Tissue overlay. Thin, translucent paper covering mechanicals both for protection and to carry printing instructions.

Title page. Page in the front of a book listing the book title, author, and publisher.

TOC. Abbreviation for Table of Contents.

TR. See Transpose.

Tracking. Text type composed with different degrees of letterspacing. Also see Minusing, Squeezing, and Kerning.

Transfer type. See Press type.

Transparency. Used to refer to a photographic slide.

Transparent ink. Printing ink that does not conceal the color over which it is printed. Process inks are transparent, thus permitting them to blend with other colors.

Transpose. To exchange the position of a letter, word, or item with another. Indicated on proofs with *tr* or the proofing symbol (t̲e̲h̲).

Trim marks. Marks placed on the mechanical to indicate the edge of the page; a guide for final cutting.

Trim size. The size of the finished item after the paper has been trimmed.

Two-sidedness. Paper having difference in appearance and printability between its top (felt) and wire sides.

Typeface. A particular style of type design including the full range of characters, in all sizes.

Type family. All the variations of a specific typeface design, such as italic, bold, extra bold, condensed, etc.

All the variations on a particular typeface, taken together, are called the type family. Here are a few members of the Helvetica family.

Helvetica EXTRA LIGHT

Helvetica LIGHT CONDENSED

Helvetica LIGHT

Helvetica LIGHT ITALIC

Helvetica MEDIUM CONDENSED

Helvetica MEDIUM

Helvetica MEDIUM ITALIC

Helvetica COMPACT

Helvetica BOLD CONDENSED

Helvetica BOLD

Helvetica BOLD ITALIC

Helvetica OUTLINE

©1976, Letraset USA.

Type high. The height of letterpress type. In U.S. .918 inch.

Type size. The size of type, measured in points. Originally, the point size referred to the piece of metal the type image was on, not to the size of the typeface itself. Now used as an approximate indication of the size of the typeface itself. For example, a 10-point typeface is ordinarily cast (in metal) on a 10-point body. While all 10-point typefaces are roughly the same size, there often is variation between faces. Also referred to as point size. (See page 45.)

Typewriter type. Typeface that imitates letters produced on a typewriter.

Typo. Typographical error.

Typography. The art and technique of working with type elements, regardless of the process used to create them.

U&LC. Abbreviation for capitals (uppercase) and lowercase letters.

Uncial. Typeface having the special characteristics of handwritten letters, based on early Latin manuscripts. Example: Unciàla.

Uppercase. Capital letters, originally stored in the upper of the two cases from which a compositor set type by hand.

Vandyke proof. Proofs brown in color; also called brownlines.

Varnish. A gloss or dull coating applied to printed sheet (or spot sections) to protect and improve appearance. Often applied on press.

Vellum finish. A toothy finish on paper, relatively absorbent to provide fast ink penetration.

Velox print. A photographic paper print made from screen negative.

Verso. Left-hand page, always even number, as opposed to recto, or right-hand page.

Virgule. See Slash mark.

Visual signal. Author's term for anything associated with a printed page that visually imparts a message to the reader.

Visual spacing. Adding or subtracting white space between type characters (or other elements), based on visual judgment.

Watermark. A design created during paper manufacture that is visible when held up to light. Paper having a custom watermark can be obtained for uses such as personal stationery. See Shadowmark.

Wax. Melted wax used to mount materials on art board when preparing mechanicals. Special rubber cement and spray adhesive are also used.

Web press. Press which prints from rolls of paper.

Weight. The degree of darkness—from black to gray—projected by a page or column of text type. Also called color.

Wf. See Wrong font.

White print. Positive duplicate of printer's negatives made on plastic sheet.

Widow. 1. A line of type (usually the last line of a paragraph) that is markedly shorter than full measure, usually two words or less. 2. A short line of type that falls at the top of a column or page. Also called orphan. Usually considered undesirable.

Wire side. On paper, produced by being next to wire during manufacture. The opposite from felt (top) side.

With the grain. Printing on or folding paper so work is parallel to the grain.

Wood type. Type made from wood, usually of large size, often used for posters, signs, etc. Measured in multiples of picas, designated as lines; i.e., 4-line (48-point), 10-line (120-point).

Word spacing. The amount of white space between words, normally ⅓ of an em for text, en space for capitals.

Wove paper. Paper having uniform unlined surface and soft smooth finish. Compare Laid paper.

Wrap-around type. Type lines adjusted to fit around a picture or other irregular-shaped graphic element.

Wrong font. Letter or character set in the wrong size or face in typeset material, marked "wf" by proofreader.

X. Used in type specifications to indicate *extra*, as in Bodoni X Bold.

X-Acto. Brand of small, sharp knife commonly used in paste-up. Often used generically to indicate any such knife.

X-height. Height of the *body* of lowercase letters, not counting ascenders and descenders.

The x-height is the height of the body of the lowercase letters.

INDEX

Other Art Books from North Light

Graphics/Business of Art

Airbrushing the Human Form, by Andy Charlesworth $9.95

Artist's Friendly Legal Guide, by Floyd Conner, Peter Karlan, Jean Perwin & David M. Spatt $18.95 (paper)

Artist's Market: Where & How to Sell Your Graphic Art (Annual Directory) $22.95

APA #2: Japanese Photography, $69.95

Basic Desktop Design & Layout, by Collier & Cotton $27.95

Basic Graphic Design & Paste-Up, by Jack Warren $14.95 (paper)

The Best of Neon, edited by Vilma Barr $59.95

Business & Legal Forms for Graphic Designers, by Tad Crawford $19.95 (paper)

Business and Legal Forms for Illustrators, by Tad Crawford $5.95 (paper)

Business Card Graphics, from the editors of PIE Books, $34.95 (paper)

CD Packaging Graphics, by Ken Pfeifer $39.95

CLICK: The Brightest in Computer-Generated Design and Illustration $39.95

Clip Art Series: Holidays, Animals, Food & Drink, People Doing Sports, Men, Women, $6.95/each (paper)

COLORWORKS: The Designer's Ultimate Guide to Working with Color, by Dale Russell (5 in series) $9.95 each

Color Harmony: A Guide to Creative Color Combinations, by Hideaki Chijiiwa $15.95 (paper)

Complete Airbrush & Photoretouching Manual, by Peter Owen & John Sutcliffe $24.95

The Complete Book of Caricature, by Bob Staake $18.95

The Complete Guide to Greeting Card Design & Illustration, by Eva Szela $29.95

Creating Dynamic Roughs, by Alan Swann $12.95

Creative Director's Sourcebook, by Nick Souter and Stuart Neuman $34.95

Creative Self-Promotion on a Limited Budget, by Sally Prince Davis $19.95 (paper)

The Creative Stroke, by Richard Emery $39.95

Creative Typography, by Marion March $9.95

The Designer's Commonsense Business Book, by Barbara Ganim $22.95 (paper)

The Designer's Guide to Creating Corporate ID Systems, by Rose DeNeve $27.95

The Designer's Guide to Making Money with Your Desktop Computer, by Jack Neff $19.95 (paper)

Designing with Color, by Roy Osborne $26.95

Desktop Publisher's Easy Type Guide, by Don Dewsnap $19.95 (paper)

Dynamic Airbrush, by David Miller & James Effler $29.95

59 More Studio Secrets, by Susan Davis $12.95

47 Printing Headaches (and How To Avoid Them), by Linda S. Sanders $24.95 (paper)

Getting It Printed, by Beach, Shepro & Russon $29.50 (paper)

Getting Started as a Freelance Illustrator or Designer, by Michael Fleischman $16.95 (paper)

Getting the Max from Your Graphics Computer, by Lisa Walker & Steve Blount $27.95 (paper)

Graphically Speaking, by Mark Beach $29.50 (paper)

The Graphic Artist's Guide to Marketing & Self-Promotion, by Sally Prince Davis $19.95 (paper)

The Graphic Designer's Basic Guide to the Macintosh, by Meyerowitz and Sanchez $19.95 (paper)

Graphic Design: New York, by D.K. Holland, Steve Heller & Michael Beirut $49.95

Graphic Idea Notebook, by Jan V. White $19.95 (paper)

Great Package Design, edited by D.K. Holland $49.95

Great Type & Lettering Designs, by David Brier $34.95

Guild 7: The Architects Source, $27.95

Guild 7: The Designer's Reference Book of Artists $34.95

Handbook of Pricing & Ethical Guidelines, 7th edition, by The Graphic Artist's Guild $22.95 (paper)

HOT AIR: An Explosive Collection of Top Airbrush Illustration, $39.95

How'd They Design & Print That?, $26.95

How to Check and Correct Color Proofs, by David Bann $27.95

How to Design Trademarks & Logos, by Murphy & Row $19.95 (paper)

How to Draw & Sell Cartoons, by Ross Thomson & Bill Hewison $19.95

How to Draw & Sell Comic Strips, by Alan McKenzie $19.95

How to Draw Charts & Diagrams, by Bruce Robertson $12.50

How to Find and Work with an Illustrator, by Martin Colyer $8.95

How to Get Great Type Out of Your Computer, by James Felici $22.95 (paper)

How to Make Money with Your Airbrush, by Joseph Sanchez $18.95 (paper)

How to Make Your Design Business Profitable, by Joyce Stewart $21.95 (paper)

How to Understand & Use Design & Layout, by Alan Swann $21.95 (paper)

How to Understand & Use Grids, by Alan Swann $12.95

How to Write and Illustrate Children's Books, edited by Treld Pelkey Bicknell and Felicity Trotman, $22.50

International Logotypes 2, edited by Yasaburo Kuwayama $24.95 (paper)

Labels & Tags Collection, $34.95 (paper)

Label Design 3, by the editors at Rockport Publishers $49.95

Letterhead & Logo Designs 2: Creating the Corporate Image $49.95

Licensing Art & Design, by Caryn Leland $12.95 (paper)

Living by Your Brush Alone, by Edna Wagner Piersol $16.95 (paper)

Make It Legal, by Lee Wilson $18.95 (paper)

Making a Good Layout, by Lori Siebert & Lisa Ballard $24.95

Making Your Computer a Design & Business Partner, by Walker and Blount $10.95 (paper)

Marker Techniques Workbooks (8 in series) $4.95 each

North Light Dictionary of Art Terms, by Margy Lee Elspass $12.95 (paper)

Papers for Printing, by Mark Beach & Ken Russon $39.50 (paper)

Preparing Your Design for Print, by Lynn John $12.50

Presentation Techniques for the Graphic Artist, by Jenny Mulherin $9.95

Primo Angeli: Designs for Marketing, $7.95 (paper)

Print Production Handbook, by David Bann $16.95

Print's Best Corporate Publications $34.95

Print's Best Logos & Symbols 2 $34.95

Print's Best Letterheads & Business Cards, $34.95

The Professional Designer's Guide to Marketing Your Work, by Mary Yeung $10.50

Promo 2: The Ultimate in Graphic Designer's and Illustrator's Promotion, edited by Lauri Miller $39.95

3-D Illustration Awards Annual II, $59.95

Trademarks & Symbols of the World: Vol. IV, $24.95 (paper)

Type & Color: A Handbook of Creative Combinations, by Cook and Fleury $39.95

Type: Design, Color, Character & Use, by Michael Beaumont $19.95 (paper)

Type in Place, by Richard Emery $34.95

Type Recipes, by Gregory Wolfe $19.95 (paper)

Typewise, written & designed by Kit Hinrichs with Delphine Hirasuna $39.95

The Ultimate Portfolio, by Martha Metzdorf $32.95

To order directly from the publisher, include $3.00 postage and handling for one book, $1.00 for each additional book. Allow 30 days for delivery.

North Light Books
1507 Dana Avenue, Cincinnati, Ohio 45207
Credit card orders
Call TOLL-FREE
1-800-289-0963
Prices subject to change without notice.